MARRIAGE

No. _____ EXPIRES _____

LUCADO, DENALYN

PROMISES, PROMISES

IS ENTITLED TO DRAW MATERIALS FROM

CARD

# Promises Promises

# Promises Promises

## UNDERSTANDING
## & ENCOURAGING
## YOUR HUSBAND

FOREWORD BY
*Denalyn Lucado*

VISION™
HOUSE
PUBLISHING, INC.

*Gresham, Oregon, 97030*

PROMISES, PROMISES
©1996 by Vision House

Editor: Liz Heaney

Published by Vision House Publishing, Inc.
1217 NE Burnside, Suite 403
Gresham, Oregon 97030

Printed in the United States of America

*International Standard Book Number:* 1-885305-39-7

Unless otherwise indicated, Scripture quotations are taken from The Bible:
The New King James Version, copyright 1984 by Thomas Nelson, Inc.

Scripture quotations marked KJV are from the Holy Bible:
Authorized King James Version.

Scripture quotations marked NASB are taken from the New American
Standard Bible, ©1960, 1962, 1963, 1968, 1971, 1972, 1973, 1975, 1977
by The Lockman Foundation.

Scripture quotations marked NIV are taken from the
Holy Bible, New International Version®. Copyright 1973, 1978, 1984
by the International Bible Society. All rights reserved. The "NIV"
and "New International Version" trademarks are registered in the United
States Patent and Trademark Office by International Bible Society.
Use of either trademark requires permission of
International Bible Society.

Scripture quotations marked LB are taken from
The Living Bible, copyright 1971
by Tyndale House Publishers, Wheaton, Ill.

96 97 98 99 00 01 02 03 04 05 - 10 9 8 7 6 5 4 3 2 1

# CONTENTS

# $\mathcal{P}$romises, $\mathcal{P}$romises

DENALYN LUCADO

$\mathcal{S}$ince I've already read this book, I want to prepare you for what's ahead. Here is what you'll need.

First, find a cozy chair, a cup of coffee, and a little time. Get ready to be encouraged, inspired, and convicted. These writers bring godly wisdom to each page—wisdom born of age, experience, and life. You will recognize many of their names (at least their last names), for they are all involved in life-changing ministries with their husbands. You have been touched by these women and possibly thought to yourself, *If I could just have an afternoon with....* Well, here is your chance. You will not be disappointed.

Second, you might grab a highlighter before you sit down. The insights these women offer are worth keeping. They've asked your questions and struggled for answers. In this book they share what they've learned in humility in order to keep their promises to God and to their husbands. None of them claim to be perfect, but all claim to be forgiven. Collectively they cast a clearer vision for women who love God and desire to serve Him more perfectly.

Third, bring a box of tissues, for these pages will touch your soul. You might brush away a tear as you're reminded of what matters in this world. As life has it, those closest to us get the worst of us. They get our bad moods, our bad breath, and our bad habits. They also get our deepest love and passion. After sitting at these women's feet, I know I can give my family more. They have reminded me that people are more important than possessions, that relationships matter more than schedules.

Keep your Bible handy. *Promises, Promises* was written to take you closer to God, the first Promise Maker. You'll see Him as the faithful Promise Keeper and the devoted Promise Seeker. He seeks a relationship with all His children based on promise and commitment. He is the God of reconciliation. He continues to search out lost souls who need a Promise Keeper. Those of us who look to God as the great Promise Maker are challenged to keep God number one on our priority list. He empowers us for this task by the Holy Spirit dwelling within us. Now we are free to keep the promises discussed in this book and to encourage our spouses to do the same.

Finally, I encourage you to bring an open heart. *Promises, Promises* is a book from the heart, a conversation from one woman to another. Whether young or old, married or single, with children or without, when women are honest with each other, something special happens. I'm praying that something special will happen in your heart.

**Denalyn Lucado** is the wife of author Max Lucado. They have three girls and live in San Antonio, Texas. Denalyn is most fulfilled in her role as mother and finds great joy in prayer and song.

# CHAPTER ONE

# What Is a Promise?

Marijean Green

$\mathcal{I}$ remember an incident that took place when I was twelve years old, an age when every child needs to feel accepted, and girls and boys are just starting to notice each other. (This was back in the '60s!) One day during recess as I waited for my turn at a game of four square, a classmate named Rose came over to stand in line behind me. She proceeded to tell me that one of the boys in our class didn't like me because I had "black teeth." She didn't know that I had been sick as a child and the medicine prescribed for my asthma had caused my teeth to discolor and turn gray. Crushed in my spirit and trying to hide my hurt, I left school feeling angry, alone, and ugly.

My mom greeted me at the door with her usual smile. "Hello, honey. How was your day?" With head low I muttered, "Fine," then headed straight for the piano. She could always tell what mood I was in by the way I played. After allowing me to vent my frustrations on the keys, she lovingly sat me down on the couch and we talked. I cried as I expressed my hurt, and she responded tenderly with a promise: "Your dad and I will do everything we can to make your smile just the way you want it, but I want you to know that you reflect a beauty that goes beyond any smile because you reflect Christ who is in you."

Her words planted hope within me. That's what promises do. They give hope.

When our daughter Summer turned thirteen, she told Steve and me that she wanted to make a commitment to the Lord to remain sexually pure. On her birthday we all dressed up and drove to Choices, a quiet restaurant in quaint, downtown Franklin. After homemade blackberry cobbler and cappuccino Steve presented her with a simple birthstone ring.

"Summer," he began affectionately, "we are so proud of you. You are a precious young lady and God has something very special for your life. In the next few years you will face many temptations to compromise your stand. This ring is a reminder of the promise you are making. Mom and I also want to make a promise to you. By God's enabling, we will always be together and are committed to love each other as long as we live."

Listening intently, Summer smiled as Steve lovingly placed the ring on her finger. What a joy it has been to see how the promises we all made that day have provided a bedrock foundation of hope in our daughter's life.

Learning the importance of promises is a daily process. Before one of Steve's concert trips, he told our ten-year-old Josiah, "Son, I want you to take care of Mom for me while I'm away. You are going to be the man of the house."

With shoulders squared and eyes peering out from under his favorite ball cap, Josiah answered, "Yes, sir. I will."

The next day Josiah asked if the two of us could go out on a date. I suggested Taco Bell, but he said that Chili's would be just fine with him. After eating our chicken fajitas, I reminded him of how Daddy helps with my coat and opens the door for me. As we left the restaurant, Josiah held the door, then put his arm around my waist and said, "I sure love you, Babes." He was playfully mimicking what he'd seen his father do many times. Josiah was fulfilling his promise to his dad.

Steve and I realize the weighty responsibility of raising our children to keep their promises. Ultimately our children become a lot like us—and we are flawed and imperfect. We have confessed to them the weakness of our human hearts due to sin. Occasionally we have had to ask their forgiveness for not fulfilling our word. Our only hope is to point them to our heavenly Father, who has never failed. Joshua 23:14 says, "You know with all your heart and soul that not one of all the good promises the Lord your God gave you has failed. Every promise has been fulfilled; not one has failed."

Jesus Christ, the Promised One, not only was the fulfillment of God's promise to us of the Messiah, but also is the One through whom all the promises of God become ours. For our own good and for His glory, God wants us to be men and women of our word. Still, our confidence is not in our ability and performance but in the certainty of our Lord. Only Jesus can transform us by His grace into a people who are a reflection of His character, a people who keep their promises.

**Marijean Green** and her family make their home in Franklin, Tennessee. She is a home-school mom, Bible study leader, domestic engineer, children's taxi service, and hesitant skier. After traveling for ten years with her husband, Christian recording artist Steve Green, Marijean has finally unpacked her suitcase and settled into the rigors and pleasures of home life.

## Questions for Discussion

1. Think of a time when one of your parents made a promise to you that planted hope within you. How did it affect your perspective, and what results did it have in your life?

2. Describe some ways that you're teaching your own children to keep their promises. Give a recent example of how your child has or has not fulfilled a promise. How did you respond?

3. Describe a time when you broke a promise to your husband or child. How did you both handle the situation?

4. What are the most important promises you've made in your life so far? What are some of the most important promises others have made to you?

5. Name some of God's promises that mean the most to you. Give a recent example of how He fulfilled one of these promises in your life.

# CHAPTER TWO

# A Wife's Role

DARLENE WILKINSON

$\mathcal{I}$ will never forget the unexpected conversation my husband and I had one evening regarding my role as his wife. While Bruce was preparing his talks for a new video series entitled *A Biblical Portrait of Marriage* he sat down next to me and asked if I would answer a question for him.

"How, as my wife, do you think you help me the most?" he asked.

"Well," I began confidently, "I guess I'd start with all the obvious things I do, like making the meals, washing the clothes, cleaning the house, and taking care of the children."

"Yes, that's true," he replied, "but if something were to suddenly happen to you, would these things cease to be done?"

Reluctantly I admitted, "No, I suppose you *could* take your clothes to the cleaners, hire a cook or a maid, and get help to care for our children; but I don't think it all would be done quite as well!" I saw him trying to suppress a smile.

Then it struck me: He was not trying to make me feel like he could get along without me, but he was about to make a point I wouldn't want to miss. For the next few moments, my husband shared that even though he could hire any number of women to accomplish the tasks I did, when it came to fulfilling my role as his wife, no other woman on the face of the earth was designed or called by God to do that except me.

I began to realize that my role as Bruce's wife consisted of more than just the typical things I did to keep our household running smoothly. That conversation began a year-long process of discovering some amazing insights.

## Looking to God's Word for Answers

If you were to stop a hundred women on the street in any city in America and ask, "What is the woman's role in a marriage?" you would probably get a hundred different answers. If you could take all those answers, lay them end to end in a huge room, and lift a secret flap on each person's response, what would you discover?

Most women probably would have based their answer on what society thinks, what television portrays, what their church teaches, what their neighbors are experiencing in their marriages, or perhaps what their mothers did as wives. But given the number of marriages that are falling apart in our society, it seems unwise to trust that these sources have provided the correct answers! It seems the further we stray from the truth, the more disastrous the results.

Before we look at what God's Word has to say about a woman's role in marriage, there are two things to consider. First, let's clarify what we mean by *role*. Throughout the course of a day, a woman will find herself assuming many different roles:

daughter, student, teacher, employee, mother, friend, club member, and so on. Each role requires her to adjust her attitudes and actions according to what is appropriate for that particular situation. For instance, we all laugh at the story about the young mother of several preschoolers who, while attending her husband's office dinner, found herself cutting the boss's meat! She was still in her "mother" role. What's appropriate for one role is inappropriate for another. Although we are always a daughter, wife, or mother, we do not actively fulfill any of these roles twenty-four hours a day. Therefore, when we talk about the role of a wife, we are referring to those important times in her life that relate to her husband alone.

Second, it is important to believe there *is* a correct answer —found in God's Word—to this question of what a woman's role is in marriage; otherwise we will try to adjust the answer according to our own experience or situation. Let me illustrate with a personal story.

When our children were very small, we noticed an unpleasant pattern of behavior developing. They would whine and become cranky whenever they didn't want to do something. I didn't want to see this behavior continue, but I had no idea what to do about it. As I asked the Lord for His answer to my dilemma, I came across this verse in Philippians 2:14: "Do everything without complaining or arguing...." The reason why we're to obey this command is given in the rest of the verse: "...so that you may become blameless and pure, children of God without fault in a crooked and depraved generation, in which you shine like stars in the universe as you hold out the word of life...."

Not only did God's Word give me direction on what to do about my children, it also showed me that obeying God's

Word had an eternal purpose: to develop God's character in us. That afternoon, I sat both our children down and shared that God had a special lesson He wanted us to learn. I put the verse into their language, and then I taught them a fun little song about grumbling and complaining, and we agreed that from that day on we were going to help each other obey this verse.

You can imagine what fun they had on occasion, reminding Mommy to "do everything without complaining or grumbling." But as I look back over those years, I see that we actually became a different family as a result of going to God's Word for our answers instead of doing what we thought might be best.

## Understanding God's Plan

As Christians we are to search out and discover the mind of God on all of life's issues. Peace and contentment come from obeying His Word. God not only has the answer to life's dilemmas; He *is* the answer. He promises, "Call to me and I will answer you and tell you great and unsearchable things you do not know" (Jeremiah 33:3).

Many people are attacking the biblical role of a wife, saying it's outdated and old-fashioned. Many women are believing the lie that fulfillment comes from living lifestyles that are independent and separate from their husbands'. But the exact opposite is true. When a woman takes an active and support-ive position as a wife, she enables her husband to become all God created him to be, and in the process God accomplishes His purposes and plan for them as a couple.

The creation account gives clear insight into God's ideal plan for man and woman and how they are to complement each other. In Genesis we read that when God saw Adam's aloneness, His solution was, "I will make a helper suitable for him" (Genesis 2:18). Notice that God did not say, "I will make a companion, lover, or colaborer for Adam," although Eve was all these things. God's choice of the word *helper* here is very important.

The Hebrew word for *helper* means "to provide what is needed or lacking." The idea is for someone to come alongside another and by her assistance and support enable that person to accomplish what could not have been accomplished otherwise. Eve was to provide what was needed for the fulfillment of God's call on her husband's life as well as on her own.

God said, "It is not good for the man to be alone." Even though Adam was busy naming every living creature and Scripture gives no indication of Adam's feeling discontent, God obviously wanted to provide something extra-special for His creation. While God created Adam out of the "dust of the ground," He created Eve from Adam's rib. The fact that God created Eve differently demonstrated to the man that this gift from God was designed especially for him. Paul confirms this in 1 Corinthians 11:9 when he says, "neither was man created for woman, but woman for man."

The first time I read this verse, I reacted negatively. In fact, I had a very honest conversation with the Lord over this issue of my role: "Father," I began, "why do I feel that You favor Your men over Your women? Couldn't you have given Sarah the vision to leave home instead of Abraham? And why couldn't Moses and his wife have held up the rod together? With few exceptions, it seems that men were chosen to accomplish all the major events of history. Even Jesus, who deeply respected the women of His day, was not led to choose any female disciples. Could it be that You created men with more ability than women?"

In His tender and loving way, God began to show me that He was not saying that men are more qualified to lead, but simply that He has called men to one task and women to another. In His perfect wisdom, God not only chose to create man and woman differently, but to place the man in leadership. God designated the man as "head" of the wife (Ephesians 5:23), and when he presented Eve to Adam, it was for a reason. He had a designated role for her as well.

In a world where everyone wants to be served, being a helper does not sound very appealing. That's why it's so important to understand three things.

## God's Purpose Is Intentional

God created both man and woman in His image and gave the command to both of them in Genesis 1:28, "Be fruitful and increase in number; fill the earth and subdue it. Rule over the fish of the sea and the birds of the air and over every living creature that moves on the ground."

God loves and values man and woman equally and desires for them to be fulfilled as individuals in order for them to be all He created them to be. However, in His wisdom He knew that, to work and move together as one, their roles would have to be different—not better than or less than, but different from each other's. When a woman realizes that she has been designated as the helper by God Himself, she can begin to sense the uniqueness and specialness of her calling.

Many years ago, when Bruce first began teaching Walk Thru the Bible seminars in local churches and Bible studies, I had the opportunity to attend with him. His giftedness as a Bible teacher was always so well received that after each session the people would swarm around him, eager to express their appreciation. As I stood there hearing all these wonderful compliments, I immediately knew how to help my husband: My job was to help keep him humble!

On the ride home Bruce always asked me what I'd thought about his delivery, how he could improve his points, and if I'd mind giving him a few helpful suggestions. Mind? Why, I had taken six pages of notes, heard every grammatical error he made, and had a dozen reasons why he should or should not have said certain things. After all, no one else would tell him the truth the way I could.

Then one evening after a particularly great lesson, before I was about to go through my two pages of critical remarks I said to my husband, "It must be wonderful to hear all those positive things people say to you when you've finished teaching." I'll never forget his response. "Well," he said, "to be honest with you, I appreciate their comments and I know they're being sincere in what they say, but I really don't pay too much attention. There's only one person whose comments I really value after I teach: *yours*. I know I can trust your evaluation of me, and you're the one I need to help me become a better Bible teacher."

Suddenly my eyes were opened to the fact that God *did* uniquely place me in Bruce's life, not to keep him humble, but to help him become the best he could be as the Bible teacher God had called him to be. You can imagine how my evaluations became less critical and more constructive after I saw the specialness of my role.

## God's Picture Is Universal

God designed the marriage relationship to be a picture to the world of Christ and His Church. The body of Christ enables the work of God to be accomplished around the world. When a believer sees the big picture of how his or her obedience to the call of God works for the good of God's ultimate purpose, there is deep fulfillment and a recognition that God's ways are perfect.

Likewise, when a woman sees the importance of her role from God's perspective, her obedience and fulfillment will be noticed by those around her. She will reflect to a watching world that it's worth doing things God's way.

Jennifer was a friend from a former church who had an exciting testimony and loved to share it. Before long, she was being asked to speak at every women's retreat and Bible study within driving distance. She enjoyed her ministry and loved seeing women come to know Christ. Her husband and three children seemed very supportive when she had to travel away from home.

As time went on, however, she began to sense that all was not well at home. During her quiet times with the Lord she became increasingly convinced that she must stop her speaking. She knew in her heart that she should discuss this with her husband but put off doing so. Finally, with great difficulty, she made the decision to say no to all speaking engagements.

Several weeks later, during a late-night conversation, her husband confessed to her that he'd been going through a very difficult period of soul-searching and had not been able to share with her how deeply vulnerable he was feeling. Her traveling had made it even harder for him to feel her love and concern at this critical time. As they talked long into the night, Jennifer admitted that she had become too caught up with the things in her own life and had overlooked the fact that her primary ministry was to "be there" for her husband first.

As Jennifer began to rearrange her life so that her husband knew he came first, an amazing transformation took place. Over the next several years, the women of the church watched in awe as Jennifer's commitment to her husband resulted in his spiritual growth. Not only did he become an elder in their church, but through Jennifer's encouragement, they began a couples' Bible study in their home that had a tremendous impact on their neighborhood.

## God's Paradigm Is Perfect

We have some good examples in Scripture of women who have helped their husbands accomplish great things for God, but one person in particular is mentioned many times as being a "helper." Do you know who it is? The Lord Himself! He is described in Psalm 10:14 as the "helper" of the fatherless; and Hebrews 13:6 says, "The Lord is my helper." Where would any of us be if it were not for the loving, compassionate help we receive from our Heavenly Father?

As God's own Son, Jesus lived His entire life in service to others and asked us to follow His example. He made it a point to share with us that the real secret to greatness is in being "the servant of all." As Jesus prepared to return to heaven, He announced to His followers that He would send them "the Helper"—the Holy Spirit—who would empower them and guide them into all truth. God does not ask us to do anything that He has not done first Himself.

Can there be any greater honor given to a parent than to hear his child say, "I want to be just like you"? Our Heavenly Father feels the same way, and perhaps we are most like Him when we serve our husbands through our roles as their helpers.

## Being a Better Helper

When Angie realized that God not only called her to be a helper to her husband but also had equipped her with the specific gifts, personality, and strengths she would need to be the perfect helper, she began to anticipate all that God wanted to do through her and her husband's lives together. She taught a Sunday school class for young married women, and one morning she decided to focus on what she'd learned about being a better helper to her husband. She encouraged the class to read and pray through the following list every day during the week ahead.

## Seven Affirmations of a Perfect Helper

I am the perfect helper for my husband, for God chose me out of all the women in the world especially for him.

I am the perfect helper for my husband, for I share his hopes and dreams and bear his hurts and frustrations along with him.

I am the perfect helper for my husband, for I bring him before God's throne in prayer every day.

I am the perfect helper for my husband, for I encourage and comfort him in strategic moments.

I am the perfect helper for my husband, for I put his sexual and emotional needs ahead of my own.

I am the perfect helper for my husband, for I love him unconditionally.

I am the perfect helper for my husband, for I enable him to become all God wants him to be and I assist him in accomplishing God's purposes.

---

The following week, Angie's class hour was electrifying as each woman shared how this little homework assignment had made a definite difference in her marriage. Many of the young women had never had any instruction on how to live out their role and had tried to do what came naturally—not usually with great results. Following God's plan made the difference.

As a result of this exercise one of the women in the class came up with this acrostic as a reminder of how she could be a helper for her husband:

H   Have dinner ready when he gets home.

E   Encourage him to talk about his life's goals.

L   Listen to him with my undivided attention.

P   Pray for him every day.

E   Embrace his ideas enthusiastically.

R   Respect him by how I talk to him and about him
     before others.

## Principles You Can Trust

Wouldn't it be great if we could turn to a chapter in the Bible that clearly listed ten ways to be our husbands' helpers? It's not that simple because God has such a Father's heart toward us that He delights in being our Helper in the process of seeking our individual answers. Every couple is unique in His sight, and He alone knows best how to direct us in our role as a wife. He does, however, give us some helpful principles on which we can base our attitudes and actions.

## Have a Gentle and Quiet Spirit

God gives wives one of the greatest secrets to being fulfilled as women: He encourages us to adorn ourselves with a "gentle and quiet spirit" which He says is very precious in His sight (1 Peter 3:4). It's also precious in the sight of our husbands as well as those around us.

Several years ago at a Walk Thru the Bible President's Council, our staff couples were having a great time interacting with our guests. After our third day together, one of the guests approached me and said, "Your staff wives are very different from most of the women my husband and I meet."

"How are they different?" I asked.

"Well," she began, "they don't come across aggressive or pushy with their husbands, and they have this spirit about them that is so attractive. I really can't explain it exactly, but it's very refreshing."

Then I asked, "Would you say they have a 'gentle and quiet spirit'?" Immediately she recognized that she was seeing this verse lived out. She was watching women "adorn" themselves with inner beauty. The Lord gives us several valuable keys to developing this inner beauty.

The first and most important key is to develop our personal relationship with God. When we spend time alone with God, our spirit remains calm and our trust in Him deepens. An intimate walk with God develops an inner beauty that makes us more lovely to our husbands as time goes on.

Another key is to watch our attitude. Being angry or unforgiving makes it impossible to have a gentle and quiet spirit. As the Lord reveals anger or unforgiveness toward our husbands or others, we need to confess it immediately and seek to restore any broken relationships. As a result, we experience a freedom and peace that radiates outward.

The third thing we need to do is to develop an attitude of gratitude toward our husbands. It's easy to take love and provision for granted, so we need to make it a point to thank our husbands for even the smallest things. Our thankful attitude is contagious as our children learn to express appreciation to their father as well.

Another key God shares with us in 1 Peter 3 is that we are to be submissive to our husband only because of our deep trust in God. We must believe, by faith, that our heavenly Father is in complete control and able to work all things together for good, even when our husband makes a wrong decision. We are assured that our pure conduct before our husband will be used by God without our even having to say a word (v. 1). It may be that God views a gentle and quiet spirit as precious because He is able to work through it to accomplish what could never be attained by our human effort.

The Proverbs 31 wife obviously accomplished much in the course of each day, yet her lifestyle reflects honor back to her husband. In fact, verse 29 records the wonderful compliment her husband paid her: "Many women do noble things, but you surpass them all."

This husband was lavish in his praise because, from God's perspective, she was worth more than rubies (v. 1). Every wife wants her husband to feel he is the most blessed man on earth. Perhaps one way to ensure he will is to ask him, "How am I doing as your 'helper'?"

Jessica's husband was a second-year seminary student, and although she felt she was doing a lot to help him, the real question was, did her husband feel that he was being helped by her? One night she asked him to tell her three things she could do that semester to help him be a better student. He was delighted with her offer and proceeded to tell her. She was surprised to discover that they were easy but unexpected things she wouldn't have thought of doing had she not asked him.

Perhaps, after reading this chapter, you find yourself understanding for the first time the significance of your role as a wife. As you accept and embrace God's plan for your life, you might like to express your heart to Him in a prayer like this:

Dear Heavenly Father,

I acknowledge that You created me for
_____ (your husband's name)
and that it's Your desire that I be his "helper"
throughout our lives together. Please forgive
me for the times I have hindered Your work in
my husband's life and our lives together by not
being willing to fulfill my role as You intended.

Help me to bring glory to You as I depend
upon Your Spirit for guidance in how to best
assist and enable my husband to be his best for
You. May we, together, accomplish all that
You desire for us as a married couple in order
to impact Your world for eternity.

In Jesus' name, Amen.

As you read the following chapters, you will hear from
women who, over the years, have learned the secrets of how
to help, assist, and enable their own husbands to accomplish
their God-given potential. Every man whom God will use to
impact the world needs a woman who recognizes the significant role she plays as his wife.

**Darlene Wilkinson** is the wife of Bruce H. Wilkinson, founder and president of Walk Thru the Bible Ministries. She serves as Prayer Coordinator of the ministry and is a graduate of Northwestern Bible College in New Jersey. She and her husband have three children and one grandchild and live in Charlotte, North Carolina.

## Questions for Discussion

1. If you were to write your job description as a "helper" for your husband, what would you include on the list? What would your husband include on the list?

2. What do you think of the statement, "When a woman takes an active and supportive position as a wife, she enables her husband to become all God created him to be, and in the process God accomplishes His purposes and plan for them as a couple"? In what ways do you see this principle lived out in your marriage?

3. Do you feel that your calling to be your husband's helper is unique and precious? Why or why not?

4. In what area do you find it hardest to be your husband's helper? Why? Create an acrostic with the word *HELPER* and list practical ways you can be a better helper to him.

5. Describe a time when your commitment to fulfilling your unique role as a wife has had an impact on people around you.

# CHAPTER THREE

# Differences Can Strengthen a Marriage

NORMA SMALLEY

While my husband Gary was a pastor in Waco, Texas, we prayed faithfully that the men in our church would make long-term promises to become more committed to the Lord, their families, and each other. One Sunday morning, almost twenty years ago, Gary challenged the men to make this commitment concerning key relationships. I was excited when he finished his message and sixty men got on their knees in front of the congregation, promising to change their lives.

Following the public commitment, however, something interesting occurred. As Gary met regularly with these men for over a year, their wives expressed deep disappointment because the men were not keeping their promise. So we started meeting as couples, but this did not seem to work either. In time we stopped believing that these men would make any lasting changes.

Then during one meeting someone shared something so powerful that the men began to turn their lives around. That night one of our good friends, Ken Nair, was visiting from California. We had asked him to speak to the group and talk about how women are more sensitive to and aware of relationships than men are. Gary had been researching other differences between men and women, and he added his insights to the discussion. From the excited response of the couples, it was clear that this information helped them gain some hope that they could make some sense out of the conflicts they were experiencing in their marriages.

Over the next few months the couples in the group reported that things were greatly improving. What had made the difference? Both the husbands and wives gained information about their spouses which caused them to let go of some false expectations. They were able to see that often their disappointments could be traced to their different styles of communication rather than to a lack of love or caring. The husbands were able to make logical sense of things, and the wives were able to see how they could help their husbands be better husbands. Those men who had not been able to keep their promise for even a week have been doing so now for over twenty years.

## Why Can't a Man Be More Like a Woman?

Since that time Gary and I have seen over and over that one of the major factors that determines whether a marriage succeeds or fails is how the husband and wife handle their differences. In fact, a majority of marital problems center on one fact: men and women are different! To begin with, every cell in a man's body is different from a woman's because of chromosome patterns. And the physical, emotional, and mental differences between the sexes are so extreme sometimes that without a concentrated effort to understand and appreciate them, it is nearly impossible to have a happy marriage.

You may already be aware of many of these differences. Others may come as a complete surprise. While there are literally thousands of differences between men and women, I'm going to concentrate on four that have helped me understand why men may have difficulty following through with their promises as husbands.

**Men tend to have a greater desire to win, and women tend to cooperate more.**

Men are usually more competitive than women. Men like to be king of the mountain. This is apparent in the way boys play; they like to win. Most of a young boy's play has to do with winning. From cowboys and Indians to the business world, men seem to get status and prestige from victory. This natural tendency can cause men to be more independent; resulting in their being more distant and aloof around others —even their families—than women are.

In contrast, women love experiencing harmony in a community, feeling connected and accepted. Researchers have noted that after age five, little girls play games and activities that require cooperation. Their games have to do with sharing and understanding each other. Whereas men tend to think about themselves and their individual goals, women seem to want connection through meaningful relationships.

In general, men don't have this same natural drive for cooperation. When two men meet, they usually ask about the other's employment. Why? To find out who has the more important job. Men get a lot of their identity from their jobs because a good job is considered a trophy of how they're winning in life.

When a husband is successful, he feels fulfilled. When he's not successful, he feels like a loser.

On the other hand, women tend to get more of their identity from whom they know. This is why, if we don't get along with our husbands and children, we may be more troubled by it than our husbands. This difference can cause tension in a marriage relationship. Let me give you an example.

While Gary was jogging one day, he decided to do something loving for me. Since we were planning to go camping that day, he remembered how stressed out I got trying to pack the camper.

"I've got a surprise for you!" Gary exclaimed enthusiastically as he walked through the door. "Instead of getting stressed out packing the camper, why don't you go out to breakfast with Helen. When you get home, we'll be all packed and can pick up the kids at school."

When he finished explaining his idea, I became very upset. I thought that he'd come up with a creative way to get me out of the house so he could pack the "right" way. That way he would win! Gary became irritated because my reasoning was so far removed from his intention. He couldn't believe that I actually thought this way. By the disgusted look on his face I knew he felt like saying, "Fine, you pack the camper and I'll go to breakfast with Helen!"

As we began to discuss how I was feeling, another important difference surfaced. In addition to feeling like he wanted to win, I also felt like he was trying to control me. This issue of control points to the second important difference between men and women.

*Men tend to want to control, and women tend to be more agreeable.*

Some researchers have found that men tend to control a conversation with their wives up to 75 percent of the time. One reason for this is that women are concerned about being connected in a relationship (e.g., talking, touching, and feeling with loved ones). When a man starts to control, a woman tends to agree and lets him win because the relationship is more important to her than winning the argument. Men want to win the argument because their natural drive is to win and control.

For example, before a man walked into our marriage group one night, he turned to his wife and said, "Okay, I was wrong. Will you forgive me?"

"What are you talking about?" his wife asked, looking confused.

"Since the group is going to ask how we're doing this week," he explained, "before we walk in, I want you to forgive me for hurting your feelings."

His wife started fuming as she realized what he was doing. "Forget it," she snapped. "I'd rather watch you try to explain that to the group!"

It actually made sense to this man to seek forgiveness at the door. However, it never occurred to him that he was controlling his wife. So when she shared what happened outside, the group devoured him. After we stopped teasing this man, we helped him understand how controlling his wife is harmful to his commitment to love her.

To further illustrate how these two differences can cause conflict in a marriage, let's go back to our small group in Waco. All the men in our group were very busy. They owned small companies, were lawyers, doctors, accountants, and businessmen. Obviously, they had to be good at winning and controlling in order to accomplish these things.

During one group meeting, we encouraged the husbands to spend at least a half-hour per day in meaningful conversation with their wives. I can remember one accountant explaining that, because of his busy schedule, the only time he had was from four to five in the morning. Amazingly, this was logical to him. Furthermore, he had difficulty understanding why his wife might not be able to concentrate that early. In fact, he even wanted to set a timer so they wouldn't exceed the time limit. He felt he'd be losing if they talked longer than half an hour.

This man's desire to win at work was keeping him from winning at home. If he was going to be a successful accountant, he had to be at work at five in the morning. If he wanted a promotion and raise, or a big Christmas bonus, he had to put in the time. Therefore, he couldn't invest a half-hour in meaningful conversation with his wife. Even though his wife was willing to negotiate with him, he was attempting to control their time together. Thankfully, the other group members helped him realize that his idea was selfish and manipulative.

In contrast, many of the women who were working outside the home were willing to adjust their schedules in order to nurture a meaningful and loving connection with their husbands. This leads us to the next important difference between men and women.

**Intimacy for men tends to involve an activity, while intimacy for women tends to involve physical touch and communication.**

Most women feel connected to their husbands through words and touch. If a man doesn't provide these two things, a woman may have a very difficult time feeling close to him. Men, on the other hand, define intimacy as doing things.

This was evident at a recent marriage seminar Gary presented. He asked for a few examples of romantic activities. One woman spoke up, "Walking hand in hand on the beach at sunset."

Gary then asked, "Is there anything your husband could do that would wreck that experience?"

"Yes," the woman quickly answered. "He could bring along his fishing pole!"

When asked why he would bring his fishing gear, the husband replied that he felt that fishing next to his wife at sunset was very intimate. But his wife had a completely different definition of intimacy. Unless she was able to hold hands and communicate she felt that he was resisting being intimate.

Why do men and women have such different definitions of intimacy? I believe the reason is explained by a fourth major difference between men and women.

**Men tend to favor the left side of the brain, while women tend to favor the right side of the brain.**

Medical research studies have shown that in the womb, between the eighteenth and twenty-sixth week of gestation, something happens that forever distinguishes the sexes. Using heat-sensitive color monitors, some researchers have actually observed what happens. A chemical bath of different sex-related hormones washes over a baby boy's brain, causing several important changes that never happen to the brain of a baby girl.

Here's a cursory explanation of what happens when those chemicals hit a baby boy's system. The human brain is divided into halves, or hemispheres, each connected by a fibrous tissue called the *corpus collosum*. The sex-related hormones and chemicals that flood a baby boy's brain cause the right side of his brain to recede slightly as they destroy some of the fibers of the *corpus collosum* that connect the two sides. One result is that in most cases a baby boy is left-brain oriented from birth. Since the left side of the brain is where language and logic operate, many men tend to be more interested in facts and information and less aware of relational needs.

What about little girls? Because they don't experience this chemical bath, little girls are much more global or "two-sided" in their thinking. While electrical impulses and messages can and do go back and forth between both sides of a baby boy's brain, those same messages can proceed faster and be less hindered in the brain of a little girl.

*Now wait a minute,* some men may be thinking. *Are you trying to tell me I'm brain-damaged?*

No. What happens in the womb is simply a beautiful picture of how men and women come equipped to specialize in two different ways of thinking. And this is one major reason why men and women need each other so much!

The left side of the brain houses more of the logical, analytical, factual, and aggressive centers of thought. In my family, it's the side of the brain that Gary reserves for most of his waking hours. Because he functions primarily out of the left side of his brain, he enjoys conquering 500 miles a day on our vacation trips and gets upset at all the cars passing us when we do make a quick lunch stop. The left side of the brain favors mathematical formulas over Harlequin romances. It stores the dictionary definition of the word *love* and can't wait to rush out and buy the latest copy of some "how to" magazine to find out the latest "fix it" technique. It memorizes batting averages and boxing scores and loves to sit for hours and yell while watching grown men crash into each other in a football game.

Women function more out of the right side of the brain which houses the centers for emotions and nurturing. Our primary relational, language, and communication skills reside on this side of the brain. In addition, the right side of the brain enables us to do fine detail work, use our imagination, and spend an afternoon savoring fine art and music.

Because the right side of a woman's brain is usually more dominant, we women may stop at roadside historical markers on purpose. The right side of the brain stores the feelings of love, not just the definition of the word; and as a result, most women would rather read a home and garden magazine than *Popular Mechanics* because it's more people-oriented.

It's easier for most women to tap into the right side of their brain than it is for men, and it's this side of the brain where the skills of building an intimate relationship reside. Most women have an intuitive desire to build meaningful relationships with the people in their lives. They also tend to have a greater capacity to recognize and nurture a healthy and intimate relationship. This means that we women carry inside us a built-in marriage manual.

Even though most men don't have all the "right-brain" relationship talents women do, they can still gain tremendous insight about relationships by learning to tap into a woman's built-in relational intuition. The key for both men and women is to recognize their uniqueness. Because we are created different, we need each other in order to grow toward maturity and balance.

So, in light of these differences, how can a woman value her husband in a way he understands and appreciates?

## Seven Powerful Ways to Help Men Keep Their Promises

Consider the average wife who has been praying diligently that her husband will change and become more relational. Finally he makes a commitment to do so. She believes that soon she'll start reaping the rewards of his new commitments. Sound familiar?

Unfortunately, these expectations don't always materialize. As we try to help our husbands keep their promises, we may feel like the two young brothers who were always in trouble. They decided to go to church and confess their sins. However, that particular Sunday a visiting pastor was preaching a fire-and-brimstone sermon. At one point the preacher pointed at the kids and shouted, "Where is God, I ask you? Where is God today in our country, in your church, and in your home?"

After the boys returned home, the younger brother locked himself in the bathroom. "What's wrong?" the older one asked. "Why won't you come out?"

"Didn't you hear the pastor?" the younger brother frantically explained. "They can't find God, and they're blaming us!"

Like these two boys who thought they were being blamed for the disappearance of God, you may feel responsible if your husband does not live up to his commitments. Before you take on that kind of responsibility, I encourage you to reflect on something very important: *It's not your responsibility to get your husband to keep his promises*. That's impossible. It's God's responsibility. But you can make yourself available to be used by God. The following suggestions can assist you.

*Remember that most men are not naturally skilled at improving relationships.*

In our small group in Waco, the wives thought the men were being uncaring because they didn't follow through on their promises. But we came to realize that it wasn't as if they were lying in bed at night thinking of ways to strain their marriage or friendships. Most of the men really didn't know how to develop meaningful relationships.

This means that your husband may have a difficult time knowing how to improve your marriage or develop better parenting skills. But as the previous chapter pointed out, you're called to be your husband's helper. "The Lord God said, 'It is not good for the man to be alone. I will make a helper suitable for him'" (Genesis 2:18). Research shows that men do not function well alone. They don't eat as well, they don't dress as well, they don't even live as long. I've come to see that one of the greatest things we do for our husbands is help them understand how to relate to us better.

Women often feel that if their husbands loved them, the men would know what they are thinking and what they need. This simply isn't true. As wives, we need to learn to speak our husbands' language; we need to be direct in our communication and tell them what we want them to do. When we want them to listen to us and not give us advice, we need to tell them so. When we want their help on something, we need to ask them directly.

My friend Suzette told me a story that illustrates this point. One day before Christmas she was getting ready to wrap some large gifts she had purchased. Earlier that day her husband had asked her if she needed some help wrapping the presents.

Because she really liked wrapping Christmas gifts, she told him no.

When she got ready to wrap the gifts, her husband was in the family room watching TV. As she began moving her packages to the kitchen table, she realized they were much heavier than she'd anticipated. As she scooted a large box by the family room, her husband glanced up at her but quickly returned his attention to the game. She began to fume inside: *Can't he see that I need some help? Why is he just sitting there? This gift is for his parents, after all!*

She spent the next hour getting more and more frustrated. Later, when she finally told her husband that she was angry at him and needed to talk, he was stunned. "Honey, I asked you this morning if you wanted my help. You said *no*. I didn't offer to move the boxes because I thought you didn't want my help."

Once she realized she wanted his help, all she had to do was say, "These boxes are heavy. Would you move them onto the kitchen table for me?"

Men need us to tell them what we need from them. I've read thousands of letters over the past twenty years that underscore this point. There is no magic pill to make a man a better father and husband. This is why the second suggestion is so important.

**Don't expect change to occur overnight—it takes time to learn how to relate to each other.**

It could take months, perhaps even years, before real changes and new patterns set in. Therefore, if after two weeks your husband doesn't seem to be staying on the right track, don't panic. Be patient.

A relationship doesn't remain static year after year. You're either growing and improving or you're going downhill. If you're not studying and learning about one another, you're bound to go downhill.

Gary and I made a commitment long ago to continue to grow in our relationship. On one occasion we decided to fast together. (This was really Gary's idea because he wanted to win and conquer the fasting experience!) So he enthusiastically talked me into it. I had never fasted before, so I wasn't sure how it would go. But because I tend to agree just to stay in harmony, I went along with the plan.

We prayed, fasted, and read the Word together from Friday night through Saturday afternoon. We also took some time to work on our marriage goals. It was like we were having our own spiritual revival. However, I was not enjoying myself because I felt forced into fasting. By late Saturday afternoon I was emotionally drained and starving. We took a break by walking around an indoor mall. Unfortunately, there was food everywhere, but I couldn't have any because we'd agreed not to eat until Monday morning. So we went back to our hotel and continued fasting and working on our marriage goals. By Saturday evening, I was starting to climb the walls. I was so hungry that it became difficult for me to concentrate. So around ten o'clock Saturday night I finally pleaded, "I've got to get food. I'm done!"

"Why should we give up now when we only have one more day?" Gary demanded. Since he had fasted before, he knew that by the third day you're not as hungry. But I was done!

"I don't know what you're going to do," I snapped, "but I'm going to eat." So I enjoyed an omelet, toast, and hash browns, despite Gary's continuous glare. He had water.

The next day Gary realized we had actually to *do* the very things we had talked about over the weekend. We had to forgive and love one another. We had to accept each other as unique individuals. After we did these things, we went home in harmony.

Sometimes you'll try new things that won't work as well as you anticipated. But if your goal is to continue learning and growing, then you both can make adjustments as needed. The best way to help you and your husband succeed during this slow process is actually through the third suggestion.

**Work toward using your differences as a way to strengthen your relationship.**

One way a woman can encourage and support her husband is to learn to value his differences, such as the left-brain bent he may have. By nature, a man's left-brain tendencies can help him make important contributions to a marriage. If a man turns his competitive nature toward building a successful relationship, the marriage can grow dramatically.

For example, if you're frustrated because your husband doesn't help enough around the house, sit down with him and tell him you need his help. Ask him to talk with you about the household tasks, each of your likes and dislikes; and make an agreement about who will do which tasks. If he's a better cook than you, he may do the cooking and you the cleanup. If you enjoy the shopping and he likes keeping the books, it's pretty clear who should do what.

Why does this work? It gives a man a clear goal and takes the guesswork out of how to please you. Once he can see the advantages of making a choice (based on the facts), he can often commit himself regardless of his feelings. In other words, even on a day when he doesn't necessarily feel like doing something (like spending a half-hour in meaningful conversation with his wife), he can still make a decision to do so.

At its roots, *love is a decision, not a feeling.* Likewise, keeping commitments is not a feeling, but a decision.

### Encourage him to join a marriage support group with you.

A small group can provide three important things for your marriage. First, it gives support, which means you get a chance to be encouraged and prayed for on a weekly basis. As a result, you have additional energy to keep moving toward fulfilling the promises you've made together. Second, it provides accountability. What's great about accountability is that since you know someone will be asking you how your week went, you're constantly working on your promises. Third, men seem to learn best by watching other men interact with their mates. If your husband came from a home where his father wasn't a model of a good husband, other men in a small group may provide healthy role models.

We have found that the most effective small group is one in which all members agree on the goals and direction. I encourage you to develop some specific goals so you don't end up forming just a social group. Also make sure your group is healthy in the sense that one person is not controlling the group or stifling your ability to grow closer to the Lord.

### Always be willing to help your husband up when he falls.

Once when we were driving back from the Arizona mountains, Gary and I got into a major conflict about where to eat breakfast. We were so angry that by the time we got to a restaurant, we weren't speaking. So we got back into our car and kept driving. One hundred miles later, Gary finally said, "I don't know if I want to continue to try. I just can't seem to get this down. I say something that makes you angry; then you say something that makes me angry. I just feel like giving up!"

Instead of thinking that everything was lost, I was able to remind him how many times we'd been successful. I knew we weren't perfect, but I knew we could keep moving. When you encourage your husband to look at the overall picture, you renew his energy. He feels like a failure when you're in the middle of a big conflict. It's as if his favorite football team has just lost. Part of your responsibility and privilege is to lift him back up and tell him you can make it as a couple. Many times I've watched Gary get encouraged and re-energized when I've taken that step.

### Pray persistently.

Luke 18:1-8 tells a story about how we should pray for one another. The word picture that Christ uses here is of a widow who never gave up pleading before a wicked judge. She kept asking every day for justice against her adversary.

After she came before the judge many times, he finally gave her justice, even though he admitted he couldn't care less for God or human beings. Why did the wicked judge grant this woman her request? Because she kept "bothering" him! Jesus concludes the parable of the persistent widow by explaining how much more our heavenly Father will give us when we "cry out to him day and night" with our requests.

Like the widow in Luke 18, we need to stand before the Lord each day, asking if today is the day He will answer our prayers. We must never give up asking the Lord to send the improvements and growth necessary to help our husbands. We must continue to ask God for wisdom and insight and for the strength to persevere. He will cause us to rise up and fly like eagles, walking and not fainting. Why? Because it is His will.

***Learn how to praise any action that brings energy or joy to you or your family.***

A man decided that he needed to be more affectionate with his wife. One day while he was showering, he realized he'd forgotten his towel. As he jumped across the hall to grab one, he saw his wife in the kitchen. Determined to keep his new promise, he decided to surprise her with a meaningful hug! So he ran into the kitchen, threw his arms around her, and shouted, "Honey, I love you!"

Everything was perfect until he heard a noise behind him. He was horrified when he turned around and saw the neighbor lady sitting at the table!

Although his wife was very embarrassed, she was able to recognize and praise her husband's positive effort. She's a wise woman. She understands that their relationship is like a bank account. Words of praise are $1,000,000 deposits. Every time you deposit something in your husband's account, it gives him energy. Every time you criticize him, valuable energy is withdrawn from the account. Unfortunately, if at the end of the month your relationship has more withdrawals than deposits, then you risk bankruptcy.

In 1 Peter 3:1–2 the Apostle says that when a man feels genuinely respected by his wife, he may be "won over" to honor God and His Word. In other words, it actually motivates a man spiritually when he sees his wife honoring him through the purity and reverence of her life. Nestled away in Ephesians 5:33, we find a very important instruction to wives: "Each one of you also must love his wife as he loves himself, and the wife must respect her husband."

Whatever we do as wives, we should never neglect to respect our husbands. That means attaching the highest value to him and treating him as a treasured person. Since a man's deepest need is to feel adequate and treasured by another human being, only we can give this special gift to our husbands. The pastor's wife, the neighbor's wife, or a single woman can't provide this. Even a daughter can't give her father the honor that a wife can.

Let me close with one more story which shows how much our husbands need and appreciate our praise. One day Gary came to my office right after I finished talking with a pastor on the phone. He threw his arms around me, kissed me, and told me how much he appreciated what I was doing at *Today's Family*. I could see by the sparkle in his eyes that he was very happy.

"Do you have any idea how wonderful I felt listening to you on the phone just now?" Gary asked. "I overheard you telling the pastor how great it would be if he invited me to his church. I heard you explaining what I teach and how much you've learned from me, how real and transparent I am, and how I live what I preach."

I had no idea that Gary was listening to what I was saying about him. But his words reminded me how much he—and all men—need to be appreciated and honored. That's their deepest need. It's what gives them energy to continue trying to be better husbands and fathers.

**Norma Smalley** was born and raised in Southern California where she attended East Los Angeles College and Biola University. She taught preschool and elementary school for five years. She and her husband, Gary, have been married for thirty-one years and have three grown children and two grandchildren. Norma is the chief administrator at Today's Family.

## Questions for Discussion

1. Name at least three ways in which you and your husband are different. Describe a situation in which these differences caused conflict, and one in which your differences complemented each other.

2. Of the four primary differences between men and women described in this chapter, which one causes the most conflict or frustration between you and your husband? What could you do in the next few days or weeks to handle these differences more positively?

3. Name several ways in which, because of your natural differences, you and your husband are uniquely skilled at strengthening your relationship. What are some specific examples of ways you've each used these skills in the past week?

4. Of the seven suggestions for how you can strengthen your marriage, which one can you use the most work on? What will you do in the week or month ahead to improve your perspective and be available to be used by God in helping your husband keep his promises?

5. What evidence have you seen in your husband that indicates that his greatest need is to be honored? What will you do this week to honor him as only a wife can?

# CHAPTER FOUR

# *Honoring Christ*

## Vonette Zachary Bright

*W*hile Bill and I were on our honeymoon, I heard words that marked our marriage and my life forever: "I want you to be your own person. I married *you*, Vonette Zachary. You are just adding *Bright* to your name. I like you the way you are and I don't want you to try to be someone else." My new husband went on to tell me he wanted our marriage to be a partnership. He told me the details of his business and said he wanted me to have a vital part in making decisions and building our relationship together.

At that moment, Bill Bright could have asked me to jump over the moon and I would have attempted it. After forty-seven years of marriage I still feel much the same way. I'm a fortunate woman with a husband who has made me his partner in life and ministry, a man with advanced ideas for his time.

When we married, Bill was twenty-seven and had achieved a considerable degree of success in business. He was also attending seminary part time. I was twenty-two and just out of college. He had been a committed Christian for three years and was growing quickly in his faith. When he received Christ, it was with a total abandon that made everything else in life secondary. Business, relationships, material wealth—all were a means to serving the Lord.

Only a few months before, I had made my commitment to Christ as a result of trying to rescue Bill from what I had wrongly concluded was religious fanaticism. The result was that he introduced me to sharp, attractive people to whom God was real and whose faith had made a difference in their lives. I had known about God all my life, but now I wanted to know Him personally. I learned that this was possible through the study of God's Word.

You can imagine, however, the potential conflicts that could arise between two newly married, strong, ambitious, materialistic, and sometimes immature people with differences of opinion. We were endeavoring to accomplish what many were sure would be an unrealized dream to reach the world for Christ, beginning with students. The Great Commandment to *love* and the Great Commission to *go* consumed our lives. We were very happy and excited about what God was calling us to do, but we also had many rough edges to be smoothed away—and God is still not through with us.

The glue that has held Bill and me together for forty-seven years is our commitment to Christ and to each other. From the earliest days of our lives together, worship, prayer, and our personal obedience to God have been the ingredients that have kept us excited about our faith, our walk, our partnership, and our ministry.

## *Worshiping God Together*

As Bill and I have studied God's attributes and spent time in His Word, we have been drawn to worship Him. We worship an all-loving, all-powerful, all-knowing, omnipresent, faithful, personal God—a God who created the universe and is interested in every detail in it but is also interested in the details in our lives. Bill and I try to remind ourselves often of the greatness of God. We acknowledge His Lordship daily.

In Mark 8:34–35, Jesus speaks to His disciples and to us: "Then he called the crowd to him along with his disciples and said: 'If anyone would come after me, he must deny himself and take up his cross and follow me. For whoever wants to save his life will lose it, but whoever loses his life for me and for the gospel will save it."

Again, in Mark 10:28–30, we are reminded that nothing matters more in this world than commitment and dedication to Christ: "Peter said to him, 'We have left everything to follow you!' 'I tell you the truth,' Jesus replied, 'no one who has left home or brothers or sisters or mother or father or children or fields for me and the gospel will fail to receive a hundred times as much in this present age (homes, brothers, sisters, mothers, children and fields—and with them, persecutions) and in the age to come, eternal life.'"

To get to know God—to understand Him—we must spend time with Him and His Word daily. Bill and I have made it a priority to spend time in worship and praise and thanksgiving every day. As our children were growing up, we worked to include them in a time of family worship appropriate to their age and interest.

One of the ways I've consciously tried to support Bill in his commitment to worship God on a daily basis is to make our home an attractive place of refuge that's conducive to worship and praise. I do everything I can to make it a home rather than an office. I also join him in listening to Scripture on tape. I have placed a tape player in our bedroom so we can listen to Scripture, to music, and even to sermons as we prepare for the day or prepare to retire at night.

Church is extremely important to us and to our staff worldwide. We both found Christ through the church. We are ministering regularly in churches and believe Scripture wisely admonishes us not to forsake our coming together in worship. There is so much to be gained and enjoyed in the company of other believers worshiping together in God's house. Our discipline and obedience in church attendance pleases God and is always rewarding to us.

## Praying Together

Throughout our marriage, our prayer life has been significant in helping us maintain consistent harmony in our relationship. When we first started dating, Bill suggested we end each date with prayer. Because we were apart during most of our courtship, he in California and I in Texas, these times of prayer about our relationship and future were very important to us. After we married, it seemed a natural continuation to pray together in the morning as we started our day and at night before we went to bed. I'm not sure we would be together today without this practice.

Of course our view of God affects our prayer life just as it does our worship. In order to pray effectively, we have to understand God's Word and we have to spend time with Him. For me, prayer is a means of developing an intimate relationship with God. In prayer we get to know God personally and begin to understand the way He works in our lives and the lives of others.

I love the following promises:

> You do not have, because you do not ask God (James 4:2).

> The prayer of a righteous man is powerful and effective (James 5:16).

> But seek first his kingdom and his righteousness, and all these things will be given to you as well (Matthew 6:33).

> Call to me and I will answer you and tell you great and unsearchable things you do not know (Jeremiah 33:3).

I am still learning so much about prayer in my walk with God, but I have come to believe that my quiet times with Him are the most rewarding way I can spend my time. The more time I spend in prayer, the more I wonder why I don't spend more time. I have learned that nothing is too great to bring before the Lord, and nothing is too small for Him to answer.

I'm constantly looking for ideas and methods to make prayer more meaningful to me and to delight the heart of Jesus. My prayers have been more focused and more effective since I started using a prayer diary. It helps me remember to pray for specific requests on certain days of the week. I've learned to pray Scripture back to the Lord by claiming specific verses for specific requests.

Both Bill and I have our times alone in prayer but there is something very special about praying together as husband and wife. When you pray together, you sense if there is a lack of harmony. Anything wrong between you hinders oneness. We have learned to be sensitive to each other, to confess to each other and to God when anything is amiss between us. We have learned to ask God what He wants for us. We ask not for what I want or what Bill wants but for what God wants for us. This kind of praying has solved conflicts and helped us through a few impasses in our relationship. We strongly advocate that you pray together as husband and wife—not preaching to each other in prayer, but communicating to the Lord and each other what is on your hearts.

Over the years I have seen that fasting can increase the effectiveness of prayer. For years I regularly fasted one day a week. Bill has fasted on hundreds of occasions, including two forty-day fasts. God has honored those times in amazing ways.

I have not always been able to join Bill in fasting, nor has God led me to, but I've always wanted to be sensitive to what God might say or reveal to Bill, as well as be an encouragement to him. I never want to stand in the way of something God has called my husband to do. While I don't need to fast with Bill to support him, my attitude and my sensitivity to his needs enables him to keep his commitment to fast.

In July of 1995 Bill asked me what I wanted for my birthday. Months before I had concluded that I wanted to spend my birthday with my husband in fasting and prayer. When I related this to Bill he was very pleased, though, I think, surprised.

On the day before my birthday a small package appeared at our front door. It contained a small vial of oil and an unsigned note explaining that the gift-giver's pastor had prayed over this oil, trusting that the use of it would bless our lives, health, and spiritual well-being. We wondered what we were to do with the oil. Secretly, I wondered if God had provided for our time with Him the next day.

My birthday was on Sunday. So immediately after church we began to listen to a compact disc I had received as a gift. It's called *The Breath of God*[1] and offers 700 scriptural promises recorded on a musical background. As we listened and worshiped, prayed, and talked together, we were spiritually uplifted.

We also were praying and fasting about our upcoming staff training. We wanted God to prepare our hearts and the hearts of the entire staff for what He had in store. As we prayed, God led us to share some personal concerns with each other. I became convicted that my perfectionism, which I'd excused as minor, had developed into a critical spirit, and God considered it a major problem. We also realized we had become careless about pleasing each other. We both began to weep and genuinely repent over the things God was revealing. This led us to a renewal of a contract to become slaves of Christ, which we had prayerfully signed before God forty-five years before.

Late in the day we were suddenly reminded of the oil. Almost at the same moment we suggested we anoint each other with it. Sound fanatical? Years ago, maybe, but for us, right then, it was so right. We made a new commitment to each other and to the Lord. If we had not set aside the day for fasting and prayer, we may never have experienced the gift that God had in store for us.

Many people have begun to see how fasting enhances the effectiveness of prayer. Some dear friends of ours attended the second Fasting and Prayer Conference in Los Angeles. They returned home determined to pray and fast one day a week. For years they had been praying for their wayward son. After the first week's day of fasting and prayer, they received a call from their son saying he had invited Christ to take over his life. The next week he shared with his business partner, who also received Christ. A few days later, the son's partner told him that he believed they were involved in a business that didn't honor God and they should get out. Needless to say, this couple is committed to fasting with prayer. In three weeks' time their prayers of years had been answered.

## Encouraging Obedience

My husband often says that he has never met an unhappy obedient Christian, nor has he ever met a happy disobedient Christian. Think about that for a moment. It is impossible to be genuinely happy when we're disobeying God. We are happiest when we're in the center of God's will, doing what He calls us to do.

God requires our obedience if we are to know the fullness of His presence and blessing. The key for me is to simply submit to the will of God—something I find possible only through the filling and control of the Holy Spirit. I cannot obey in my own strength; I only become resentful, reactive, and frustrated when I insist on my own way.

This is true in every area of my life, and specifically in my marriage. I've been greatly helped by the practical guidance in Ephesians 5:15–33 and 6:1, which tells us how to live the Christian life on a daily basis: how to relate to God, how to relate to each other, how to relate as husbands and wives, parents and children. Interestingly, we are told to submit to each other. I am to submit to you as a believer. You are to submit to me. This means we consider each other more important than ourselves. Wives are told to submit to their own husbands. Husbands are told to love their wives as they love themselves and as Christ loves the Church. The husband described in this passage is not a demanding male chauvinist but a loving man committed to his wife's well-being and fulfillment. He is kind, protective, and encouraging, and I like to think he makes her a partner in his life pursuits. It's easy for a woman to submit to a man like that.

Recently a young feminist mother observed her stepmother being very attentive to the needs of her father. She described her stepmother as a slave to her father. The man defended himself by saying, "Yes, she is my slave, if you want to put it that way. I'm her slave, too. We're committed to doing what we can to meet each other's needs and to making each other happy."

The Bible is God's textbook for daily living. We only have to follow its instructions. God never promises us that obedience to His Word will ensure that our lives will be free of conflict. But when we are walking in the Spirit and allowing Jesus Christ to empower us, we find joy in our lives no matter what the circumstances. I'm not talking about being resigned to situations. Sometimes we need to take the initiative to bring about change. What's essential is that we submit first to God in obedience, and then leave the results in His hands.

I've found that the best way I can support Bill in his relationship with God is to join him wholeheartedly in a daily lifestyle of worship, prayer, and obedience to God. As a result, God continues to bless us with a productive and meaningful marriage and ministry. For us, it's the only way to go!

### Notes

[1] *The Breath of God.* Narrated by Chuck Millhuff, produced by Jerry Nelson. (Brentwood, Tenn.: Brentwood Music).

**Vonette Zachary Bright** was named 1995 Christian Woman of the Year and is the co-founder of Campus Crusade for Christ. Since 1971 her primary ministry has been the mobilization of prayer, first in the U.S. and then around the world. In 1993 she founded *Women Today International* and has a national radio program called *Women Today with Vonette Bright*. She and her husband, Bill, have two children and three grandchildren.

## Questions for Discussion

1. Do you agree that worship, prayer, and personal obedience to Christ are critical factors in keeping a marriage strong and happy? Why or why not? Where are you and your husband in making these factors priorities in your relationship?

2. In what ways do you and your husband join forces in ministry? What impact has your partnership in ministering to others had on your marriage?

3. What are some specific ways you might join together as husband and wife in the week ahead in the areas of worship, prayer, and obedience? Is one of you stronger in each of these areas than the other? If so, how might you encourage each other?

4. Is prayer an activity that comes naturally to one or both of you, or is it difficult? What are some specific things you do, or might try, to make prayer more meaningful and effective for you and your husband?

5. What does it mean to you to "submit" to your husband? Describe some ways you've submitted to each other in the past week. What was the result?

# CHAPTER FIVE

# *Benefiting from Vital Relationships*

## JEANNE HENDRICKS

*I*, *Jeanne, take thee, Howard, to be my lawfully wedded husband, to love and to cherish in joy or in sorrow . . . sickness or health . . . poverty or plenty . . . 'til death do us part.*

More than anything else in the world I wanted to belong to Howie, to be part of his life, from the most public to the most private. I was eager to buy the whole package—whatever it cost. It certainly sounded do-able; in fact, it sounded like a lot of fun. Howie and I could do anything, as long as we were together.

But *together* hung on a few mutual promises. Slowly I realized that the core question was not, *Will we have a happy life together?* but, *Could we follow through on those demanding vows?*

Soon I will have invested a half-century in this man with whom I stood in the warm euphoria of that June night. Sometimes we have been more "together" than others; sometimes keeping the promises we made seemed unfair, unrealistic, and even impossible. Yet we have made it through the dark tunnels and now find ourselves melded into a unity of loyal love we didn't know existed.

Apparently I'm one of the fortunate few long-marrieds. Most surveys of married couples lead to a sobering conclusion: half of all marriages fall apart, and, according to counselors, of those who stay together legally, less than one-fourth can be described as content or fulfilled.

What gave stability to Howie's and my marriage? I'm convinced that we owe a lot to what we learned from people who could teach us what we needed to know. We benefited from the example of some wise mentors who taught us the importance of strengthening each other with a braid of three strands: mutual accountability, mutual affirmation, and a shared spirit of hope and goodwill.

## Mutual Accountability Before God

Today it's all too common to hear a wife say, "Me, be accountable to him when he's clearly making a mistake?" or "Me, affirm him when he's pursuing selfish goals?" But today's widely-practiced, 50-50 approach to marriage can never fulfill two thinking adults long-term. No wonder so many marriages fail.

Ultimate satisfaction comes not by pleasing myself, but from a persistent effort to help my mate become a better person. If I focus on my resentment or how I can even the score, I will be tempted to opt out, justifying my actions: "Yes, I promised I'd be there, but he's not the same person I married!"

Marital discord has a long taproot. It reaches all the way back to the Garden of Eden where God established monogamy: equal partners, complementary roles, and Himself in the center. God said that it was not good for Adam to be alone, so He made a woman as the man's counterpart, companion, and wife.

This first marriage began in total bliss, but the crucial element was God's presence with the couple and His authority over them.

When Adam and Eve acted independently of their Creator, everything went downhill. Marriage became a head-to-head competition, and eventually both husband and wife lost the prize of a satisfying relationship. Mutual accountability is a farce unless each mate is first in tune with his or her Maker.

Holding oneself accountable to another person is like stepping up the rungs of a ladder. We have a solid foothold only if that ladder is leaning against a reliable wall. Mutual accountability works when each partner is solidly resting against the trustworthy presence of the One who brought them together. Only then is the emotional and relational ladder manageable over the years.

Two couples I know illustrate this truth. Don and Jane seemed to have an ideal marriage for many years. He was an airline pilot and she and their two children enjoyed time with her parents when he was away on trips. In their middle years, however, a child with Down's syndrome was born to them. As the older children married and left home, the unrelenting stress of caring for a child who could not develop normally strained and eventually broke their marriage.

Although both Don and Jane were Christians, they could not weather this major storm in their lives. Each one secretly blamed the other for what they considered to be a major misfortune. They were not able to trust in God's provision of strength for their difficult journey.

Jim and Ann, in contrast, reared two children while also building a successful family business. Both of the children apparently felt neglected and decided to reject their parents'

Christian values. When Jim and Ann discovered that their grandchildren were virtually homeless, without caring, concerned parents, they began to nourish and to parent their grandchildren, at a great personal sacrifice. Their marriage is stronger than ever as they have trusted God and each other for daily strength. Mutual accountability means committing to a team where God Himself calls the plays.

## Mutual Affirmation

Caring affirmation means doing what is best for my partner. My parents modeled this second principle, which stabilized my marriage to Howie. A couple of memories stand out in my mind. Dad was a do-it-yourself-er who loved to tinker with his car. A cold greasy garage was the last place Mother was eager to go, but out of her love for my father she often stood by the car, dutifully handing Dad one tool after the other, chatting with him all the while. She said she was "keeping him company."

For his part, Dad readily cracked walnuts for her, mashed her potatoes (by hand!), and washed her windows. He helped her by teaching me to hang a sheet outside on a windy day and how to iron his shirts. My parents affirmed each other. Is it any wonder that I'm always looking for reasons to be with my husband? For me, it's a family tradition.

As newborn babies we have a critical need to know that our world is safe, that we are accepted into it, that we are loved. Otherwise, a protective emotional skin grows, a distrust of people, an avoidance of close relationships. We carry on lifelong search for those who will affirm our worth; many of us find one special person in marriage. This one-flesh relationship probes into our deepest selves, and if at bedrock level we find mutual nourishment, then a partnership of deep respect and support flourishes. We credit each other for our strengths and assist each other with our weaknesses. We allow God's commands to govern our joint cooperation and we forgive when we overstep our boundaries.

As a teenager I watched my cousin Richard marry beautiful Franny in a storybook wedding ceremony. Only months later Franny was stricken with polio and confined to a wheelchair. I wanted to accuse God of making a terrible mistake! But Richard built her a house to accommodate her limitations and faithfully arranged his life to conform to hers, even after she became a bedridden invalid. One Valentine's Day *The Philadelphia Inquirer* headlined Richard and Franny's fiftieth wedding anniversary as an unprecedented love affair.

Shortly before Franny died, I visited Richard and asked about this amazing love. I'll never forget his response: her illness only served to bring them closer. As he lovingly cared for her, she in turn affirmed his every move and never failed to express her devotion. Most important, they each saw themselves as representations of God's love to one another. To me, their marriage was a beautiful reflection of Christ and His Church. He freely gave His love to her and, although she was totally helpless, she responded with wholehearted devotion.

Caring affirmation means always doing what is best for my partner. A devoted wife will validate every effort her husband makes to be a trustworthy man. As only a female can, she will lead him by serving, challenge him by her own chaste life, and teach him the gentle skills of tender caring by listening carefully to him and wisely interacting with him about his concerns.

## Hope and Goodwill

Husbands and wives do, of course, slip into dissonance as they face differences and resolve conflicts. But this is not only normal—it can be used for good. Discord can be part of the polishing that results in goodwill.

Howie hates it when I move the furniture around or leave a light on or a closet door open. He bristles when I'm late. These are the "little foxes that ruin the vineyard," as Solomon wrote in his Song. Love demands patience and discipline to change little things, but larger disagreements often seriously divide us. We may need to seek outside help, for example, if we can't bring our financial heads together.

Other differences are irreconcilable. In their book, *Opposites Attack,* Jack and Carole Mayhall remind us that God gave us two eyes to see things with dimension. How we talk, act, and react often clash head-on. But when we know that we can disagree and still be friends, when we work through our biases, forgive each other, and demonstrate our flexibility, then a spirit of hope pervades our home.

Jesus Christ gave us the key to goodwill. He is described in the Gospel of John as "full of grace and truth" (John 1:14). To the extent that we imitate Him, our relationships will thrive. When I as a wife graciously work to fit in with Howie's plans and submit to his wishes (without compromising my person-hood) because I want our union to be healthy, then our future together is reinforced with energy and hope.

## Mentoring Others in Relationship Skills

As I reflect on the importance of mentoring relationships in my life, I am more convinced that I have a responsibility to mentor others. I believe that stability and vitality in the home stem from the fierce determination of a wife to use her inborn strengths of loving influence to mentor those around her with godly wisdom. As Christian women, we can give direction to others and encourage and support our husbands to do the same.

Mark Twain wrote of his mother who courageously faced down a bully in their small Italian town. The man was widely known to beat his daughter when she displeased him. One day the terrified girl came running down the street with her cursing father chasing her with a rope. Twain's mother stepped out and pulled the girl into her doorway. Instead of closing the door, she stood with her arms crossed, barring the entrance. Without flinching, she stared into the father's face and rebuked him in words audible only to the man's conscience. He asked her pardon and handed her the rope, and then with a loud, blasphemous oath called her the bravest woman he had ever met. Thereafter no problems occurred, and, said Twain, his mother and the man became good friends. He had finally met a woman who wasn't afraid of him. He had risen to her standards.

Nations grow only as families flourish, and families wilt and die unless the powerful mentoring capabilities of women enrich them. As emotional caretakers, gifted by the Creator to share their maternal advantage, women can challenge men to be decent and upright.

I have seen firsthand how one woman can change the course and direction of a man's life. The man who stood at the altar with me was born to young parents who knew little beyond selfish gratification. Their new baby increased the tensions between them to the point of permanent separation.

Unwanted and uncared for, Howie landed literally in the lap of his overworked grandmother who struggled with multiple problems: loss of a son, demands of an adopted niece, and an alcoholic husband—all with the backdrop of a national economic depression. Howie's chances of being mentored into a successful and productive man were slim. Only one spark of hope flickered: Grandmother Cora sought divine help. She turned to God to supply her needs, to help the helpless. And He can be trusted to follow through.

The ministry of a small neighborhood church helped Cora grow in her faith. A Sunday school teacher led Howie to faith in Christ, and as she prayed, a series of miracles transformed him into a young man who followed God's guidance and established a Christian home, thus breaking the generational patterns of a fractured family. These godly women made a radical difference in the life of one young man.

I say all this to stress the importance of vital relationships in our lives. Both Howie and I—and our marriage—benefited from other people's input in our lives. The importance of these mentoring relationships has remained a constant throughout our lives. As women we have an inborn capacity to nurture—to mentor—and I challenge you to form relationships with other women in which you can teach what you have learned.

The young pastor, Titus, was charged with the task of establishing leadership on the island of Crete, a first-century spiritual sinkhole populated with social outcasts (Titus 1:10-14). In his letter of instructions, the Apostle Paul saluted the virtue of mentoring by older women. He instructed Titus to teach the older and younger men, as well as the older women. But he was not to teach the young women. Why? There are, of course, the obvious sexual pitfalls, but the overriding reason was that the older women are well-styled for the curriculum: "They can train the younger women to love their husbands and children, to be self-controlled and pure, to be busy at home, to be kind, and to be subject to their husbands..." (Titus 2:4–5). Where better to learn than side-by-side with a woman who herself has struggled with these challenges?

If a young woman does not know how to organize her home, if she resents cooperating with her husband, she tends to complain. Her stress prompts her to call for help. Reading or listening to principles often compounds her frustration, but when another woman shows her personally how to use her resources and how to interpret the husband-wife relationship, when she patiently encourages her to follow God's plan for living, then changes often come. Moreover, the odds are heavily in favor of her husband's responding with deep admiration.

## Encouraging Your Husband to Build Relationships with Other Men

A wise wife will encourage her husband to sustain mentoring relationships with other men. A wife who empowers her husband to be the best man he can be also influences the world outside her home as her man touches the lives of other men and reproduces the spirit of love and peace he learned at home. A wise wife realizes that her husband needs strong male friendships to balance and complement the relationship he has with her, and she is eager to encourage him to take what he's learned in their marriage and use it for good in other relationships.

The Bible warns wives that a husband is never too spiritual, too old, or too good to do something foolish. Abraham, who is called the "friend of God," succumbed to the temptation to lie about his wife, Sarah, when he was an old man—a replay of

77

the same sin he committed years before in Egypt. Moses, the meekest man who ever lived, yielded to a fit of anger and never entered the Promised Land to which he led the Israelites. Noah, after years of faithful obedience, engaged in immorality in his later years. David, the "man after God's own heart," committed adultery and murder.

How can a wife fortify her husband against foolishness and motivate him to establish strong, honoring friendships with other men? Let me suggest five qualities key to your part in a good marriage and explain how they ripple beyond your home.

### Be a Good Friend.

A pleasant, reliable friendship generates warmth and positive energy in a man. It anchors him emotionally and minimizes the brooding sadness that often precipitates rash acts.

### Be a Faithful Lover.

When a man is loved well by the woman to whom he has given everything, his natural appetite for sexual intimacy is satisfied, and he has no need to prove his manhood by illegitimate means.

### Be a Woman of Excellence.

Proverbs 31 describes this woman as more valuable than the most precious gems. Her husband has full confidence in her and he lacks nothing of value. With an asset like this woman, a husband naturally holds his head high and tries hard to live up to her confidence in him.

### Be a Fascinating Person.

As a wife reads, grows, and expresses herself with originality, her husband is stimulated to know her better and to show her off to his friends.

### Be a Godly Woman.

All of the charm and beauty a woman may have amounts to nothing if her ambitions are self-centered. But if she reflects her Creator and assumes the posture of a graceful servant, she cannot help but command high respect and favor.

All of these qualities—friendship, faithfulness, excellence, charm, and godliness—have a transforming power which inevitably is converted into masculine vitality as they are absorbed in a love relationship where trust and commitment rule. A husband with this kind of a wife conveys to his male associates a healthy confidence, reproducing the core dynamic of his own spirit.

## Our Inestimable Privilege

In her book *The Confident Woman*, Ingrid Trobisch writes of the Kiga tribe in East Africa that calls God by the name *Biheko*. The word means "a God who carries everyone on His back." In their tribe only mothers and older sisters carry children on their backs.[2] It is a picture of the inestimable privilege Christian wives enjoy: mentoring others and in so doing, demonstrating to the world how to reach out, even as did God Himself when He gave His Son.

Jehovah promised a Savior, and He kept His promise. "For to us a child is born, to us a son is given, and the government will be on his shoulders. And he will be called Wonderful Counselor, Mighty God, Everlasting Father, Prince of Peace" (Isaiah 9:6). He provides His authority and His omnipotence to enable us to build a steadfast marriage. We trusted God to keep His promises, and nothing surpasses the power of a promise kept.

## Notes

[1] Jack and Carole Mayhall, *Oposites Attack*, (Colorado Springs: Nav Press, 1990).

[2] Ingrid Trobisch, *The Confident Woman*, (San Francisco: Harper San Fransisco, 1993).

Jeanne Hendricks is a public speaker who travels worldwide and the author of several books. She is married to Howard G. Hendricks, Chairman of the Center for Christian Leadership at Dallas Theological Seminary. Howard and Jeanne have four adult children and six granddaughters.

## Questions for Discussion

1. Of the three "strands" that strengthen a marriage, which one is the strongest in your marriage: mutual accountability, mutual affirmation, or shared hope and goodwill? Which one(s) need(s) to be strengthened? Name some specific ways you might work on this in the week ahead.

2. What are some of the "little foxes that ruin the vineyard" in your marriage? Describe some ways you and your husband have successfully kept these from dividing you.

3. What do you think of the statement, "Nations grow only as families flourish, and families wilt and die unless the powerful mentoring capabilities of women enrich them. As emotional caretakers, gifted by the Creator to share their maternal advantage, women can challenge men to be decent and upright." How have you seen this to be true in your family?

4. Describe the influence of a woman in your past who mentored you in a life-changing way. Are you involved in mentoring other women? Why or why not?

5. What is the most important thing someone has taught you about how to strengthen your marriage? What are some of the things you've learned that you can teach others?

6. What specific things can you do to encourage your husband to benefit from vital relationships of his own?

# CHAPTER SIX

# Practicing Purity

CINDY TRENT

Allen had begun a new job at a company where networking was very important. One Saturday a group from the office invited him to play golf. Then they called the next week. Then, a third Saturday in a row. While his wife was happy Allen was bonding with those at his new job, Meagan felt his attention and commitment to her and the children was being directly affected.

*Should she say something to him?*

When Lisa and Steve trusted Christ, one of the first things they did was throw out Steve's *Playboy* magazines. For years he hadn't brought any home. But now, Lisa began to notice that Steve was consistently watching network television programs that were as graphic as many of the magazines he used to own.

*How should she go about talking to him about it?*

Brian works hard at a construction job where he's the only Christian on his crew. While he's worked hard to be a good witness, his wife Susan notices that lately he's bringing home tools from the site that he doesn't return and "scrap" materials that really aren't "scrap."

*How can she help him return to a commitment of ethical purity, without seeming judgmental or condemning?*

Should Christian wives actively encourage purity in their husbands' lives? Is it right for us to confront our husbands when we see things in their lives that are of potential or real concern? Or should we just stand back and pray that God will make them into men of purity?

The answer to these questions is *yes, yes,* and *yes!* Yes, we should actively encourage our husbands to be pure. Yes, it is biblical for women to confront their husbands. And yes, we should pray fervently that apart from anything we say or do, God will move our husbands toward purity—even if it means laying out what Chuck Swindoll calls "a divinely inspired obstacle course" to help them arrive there!

Scripture tells us the greatest earthly love story of all, the Song of Songs, in which a woman encourages her husband to protect their relationship from impurity and problems. There a wise bride makes a very direct request of her wise husband: "Catch for us the foxes," she says to Solomon, "the little foxes that ruin the vineyards, our vineyards that are in bloom" (Song of Solomon 2:15).

Solomon's bride isn't urging him literally to go fox hunting; she's using a word picture to confront him with the nature of their relationship. The fox is a small, innocent looking animal that is actually a cunning predator, and the vineyard is their relationship. There's trouble afoot.

This woman sets an example for Meagan, Lisa, and Susan—indeed, for all of us. There was nothing wrong with their husbands going golfing, watching television, or bringing home legitimate "scrap" materials. But in the above cases, those behaviors had begun to cross the line. They were becoming "foxes" that, if left unchecked or ignored, would begin tearing up their relationship.

Like a thriving vineyard, a life of purity must be protected or it won't remain pure. A commitment to purity means recognizing and catching moral and ethical lapses while they're still catchable "foxes" instead of letting them grow into relationship-threatening "lions."

In this day and age, a commitment to purity isn't optional —it's essential. It's a key to seeing God clearly. "Blessed are the pure in heart, for they will see God" (Matthew. 5:8). Unfortunately, in our society the word *purity* isn't used very often except on Ivory soap labels or pure vanilla extract. If we're to help our husbands and ourselves live pure lives, we need to understand what Scripture is asking us to do. So, let's begin with a definition, and then look at five clear ways purity was reflected in the life of one godly man.

*The New Bible Dictionary* gives the best definition of purity I've seen: "[Purity is] the renunciation of sin and the obedience to God which brings every thought, feeling, and action into subjection to Christ. It begins within [your heart], and extends outwards to others in every area of your life."[1]

Purity, then, is a wholehearted commitment to honoring Christ in all our thoughts and actions. This is a formidable goal, but not an impossible one.

## Five Marks of a Pure Life

Let's study a man who experienced many challenges to his commitment to purity yet remained pure: Joseph. The youngest of eleven brothers, he was tossed into a pit and sold into slavery, yet as a result he landed right in the center of God's plan to save an entire nation. A close examination of his life reveals five principles that put purity within reach for us as well.

### A person of purity deals with hardship in a God-honoring way.

Joseph certainly did. He could have seen himself as a victim and spent his life angry, whining, or defeated. But he didn't. Whether he was battling false accusations or bearing up under terrible prison conditions, he never hid behind helplessness. He never complained or ducked responsibility.

What does this mean for us? When we see our husbands bearing up well under hardship instead of backbiting, grumbling against God, or blaming others, we can affirm them for reflecting one clear mark of purity. And when we trust God with trying circumstances ourselves, we can affirm ourselves as well.

### A person of purity recognizes and flees from sexual temptation.

With the incredible amount of sexually explicit material in our culture today, sexual purity is more of a battle than ever. Yet, here again, Joseph models purity.

In the book of Genesis, we're told that Joseph was continually bombarded by sexual temptation. As the overseer of a household, he soon became the focus of an immoral woman's attention. Potiphar's wife noticed that Joseph was handsome and talented, and brazenly said to him, "Come to bed with me!" (Genesis 39:7). Though she "spoke to Joseph day after day, he refused to go to bed with her or even be with her" (v. 10).

Can you see the boundaries this godly man drew around immorality? In spite of daily pressure to cave in, Joseph refused to be sexually immoral. Later, he even put on his track shoes and fled from this temptress rather than compromise his purity.

The application for wives is clear: when we see our husbands turning off the television set when an inappropriate program comes on, making a firm decision not to watch a certain R-rated movie, or making a special effort to keep appropriate boundaries with women where they work, they deserve our praise and encouragement for fleeing temptation.

Our husbands deserve our help as well. We can make our homes as free of sexual temptation as possible. Clearly, the absence of immoral materials doesn't guarantee purity of heart, but keeping our eyes clear is an important aspect of purity (Luke 11:34–36). We can:

- Go through the magazines on our coffee table or night stand and toss out any material that downgrades purity (like the "soft porn" lingerie catalogs that are mailed in bulk).

- Be sure we don't give our husbands a double message by urging purity for them, and then reading racy romance novels ourselves. (This also goes for watching television programs centered on sexual themes, or spending inappropriate time with male friends at work, church, or social gatherings.)

- Follow the Apostle Paul's wise counsel to regularly have sexual relations with our husbands (1 Corinthians 7:3–5). In addition, we can strive to be as attractive as we can in every way.

Sexual purity in our over-sexed society takes hard work. But it's an important part of keeping the promise of purity.

**A *person of purity trusts God, not others, to advance his or her position.***

Joseph demonstrates another characteristic of purity by refusing to stoop to arm-twisting, manipulating, or using others to advance his position. That doesn't mean he didn't make friends or ask for help when he needed it. Joseph made friends with both a baker and a butler in prison, and pointedly asked if they would remember him to the Pharaoh and help him get a pardon. Neither one did for many, many months.

Did Joseph become bitter when his "friends" failed to deliver what he'd hoped? Absolutely not. He kept entrusting himself to God to advance his position in life rather than depending on his human connections.

Don't get me wrong. There is nothing wrong with building relationships or using networking to reach our goals. But a person committed to a life of purity doesn't attend church in order to make business contacts or lead a home Bible study group so that the first topic of study can be a multi-level marketing plan. Neither does he compromise his ethical standards in order to advance in his company.

Our husbands deserve our praise every time they take the high road of trusting God to advance their careers. And whether or not we have a career outside the home ourselves, we need to trust God in this area as well. Some women can be very manipulative in working their way up through the ranks of a volunteer or school organization for their own gain, not that of their child, school, or charity. Just like our husbands, we need to ask God regularly to examine our motives. While it is godly to want to do our best and be all we can be in Christ, it is ungodly to be motivated by pride, greed, or personal gain.

*A person of purity stands before his peers and superiors and courageously maintains his faith in God.*

When Joseph did get his chance to stand before Pharaoh, he did something that wouldn't have scored points with the horde of magicians and soothsayers that surrounded the court: he unashamedly claimed Almighty God as the source of his power and strength. That courageous commitment to claiming the true source of his power also reflects a life of purity.

There are times when standing up for our faith can prove costly. Recently, I saw a clear example of just such a price tag. My good friend Pam had applied for a prestigious volunteer job with the local police department that required extensive testing. For many law students, it was a crucial stamp on their resumes, so Pam joined over 120 applicants in the competition for the twenty volunteer spots available.

Pam achieved top scores at each level of testing and assessment. There was only one hurdle left, a mere formality in most cases: she had to give a final interview before the entire selection committee. The question-and-answer time couldn't have gone better; that is, until the very end. In the course of the interview, she had mentioned that she'd lost her father the year before. It was a difficult loss, and they asked her, "What was it that helped you the most in dealing with your pain?"

Without hesitation, she answered the question by talking about her faith in Christ. Instead of hedging and taking the safe or politically correct route by talking in generalities, she clearly stated that her greatest comfort came from praying to her heavenly Father. This wasn't what the panel wanted to hear. They came back with the question, "Do you feel you're applying for this job so you can share you faith with everyone you meet?" She answered that she wanted the job to help others, but she wouldn't deny the role her faith played in her life.

Pam walked away from the interview believing she had lost the job, but knowing she hadn't compromised who she was or what she stood for in Christ. When the time came for the winning applicants to be called, to Pam's surprise, she got the job! Out of the 120 applicants, her name was at the top.

Pam not only stood her ground in front of others, she gained an even deeper level of love and respect from her husband. Her boldness in sharing Christ, no matter the cost, inspired him to be even more open about his faith with others. When we get the opportunity to identify with Christ, and choose to do so, we reflect the purity God asks of us.

### A person of purity shows compassion to his loved ones.

Genesis 50 contains one of the most touching stories in Scripture. Joseph has already rescued his father and brothers from starvation by selling them grain. Then, he reveals himself to his long-lost family and brought them all to Egypt. Now his father had died and his brothers were filled with fear—and with good reason. After all, they had sold Joseph into slavery years before. Now he was one of the most powerful men in the country. What would he do to them?

If he had felt hatred or bitterness over what they had done to him, now was the time Joseph could have exacted his revenge. Instead, he extended forgiveness and compassion. When they begged him to treat them kindly, Joseph was cut to the heart and replied, "'Don't be afraid. Am I in the place of God? You intended to harm me, but God intended it for good to accomplish what is now being done, the saving of many lives. So then, don't be afraid. I will provide for you and your children.' And he reassured them and spoke kindly to them" (Genesis 50:19-21).

What a forgiving and God-honoring response! Instead of hating his brothers, Joseph expressed compassion for them. That's a mark of purity. A pure walk before the Lord doesn't allow for the darkness of anger and resentment (1 John 2:9-11).

When we see our husbands offer forgiveness to someone at work who doesn't deserve it or when they choose to forgive an offense from the past, they're practicing purity. And that's something that needs to be praised.

As wives, we too must offer forgiveness and kindness to our spouses, family members, and others as part of living out a life of purity. Stop right now and ask yourself, "Have I forgiven those who have offended me?"

If we seek to live out these five character traits amidst the bumps and bruises of everyday life, we'll live lives of purity as Joseph did. But how can we practically step up to such a challenge? I recommend four specific ways to make a commitment to purity a part of your regular practice.

## Four Ways to Encourage a Commitment to Purity in Your Home

### Praise your husband when he takes positive steps toward godly purity.

I've said this earlier, but it's so important it bears repeating. If you're serious about helping your husband (and yourself) live a life of purity, then be sure to praise him when his life reflects one of the five marks of purity. Tell him it isn't his bank account, biceps, or the letters behind his name on a business card that spark your passion—it's his commitment to purity.

But don't stop there. Be proactive in pointing out any positive steps he takes toward purity and integrity. And don't set such unrealistically high standards before you praise him that you never do! Praise your husband when he takes even small steps. You're not just inflating his ego, you're encouraging his obedience to Christ.

### Help your husband by modeling purity.

Years ago, we were having dinner with two of our special friends, Barb and Gary Rosberg. We asked them the "How did you two meet?" question, and were rewarded with a wonderful story about how one woman's integrity and commitment to purity positively—and eternally—affected her husband's life.

When they met, Gary was the fraternity man on their campus. He was handsome, intelligent, well-liked, and a party animal with a very different set of morals from Barb's. When he first saw her, he was smitten and asked her out on a date. Barb agreed to go out "as friends." But as they continued to date, and when he began to get serious, she made a decision not to compromise her personal standards or change the commitment she had made to marry a Christian.

After much prayer and thought, she broke up with Gary just when he thought he'd found the woman he wanted for his wife. While she had talked about her faith since their first date, she explained again that she couldn't date him anymore or get serious with him because he didn't personally know Jesus Christ.

Gary walked away totally confused and bewildered. No one he'd ever dated had the commitment to purity Barb reflected, nor drew the line at his lack of faith. Instead of making him angry, it drove up his interest! He was so impressed by her stand for Christ that he shocked the other guys in his fraternity by showing up at a Bible study. He wanted to know what Barb had that he didn't.

After weeks of attending that study and a nearly non-stop spiritual struggle over committing himself to Jesus, Gary finally took a long walk one night and gave his life to Christ. As he was walking back to the fraternity house to call Barb and tell her what had happened, he nearly walked right into her! Before he could even tell her, she looked at him and exclaimed, *"You became a Christian!"*

A few months later Barb and Gary were engaged, and now they've been married for over fifteen years. Today they have an outstanding Christ-centered marriage and family, and I'm convinced that it began when Barb committed herself to a life of purity.

Please don't misunderstand. I'm not saying that if you commit yourself wholeheartedly to Christ and to a pure life, your non-believing friend or spouse will automatically come to know Jesus. In fact, some husbands may even become defensive or even outright antagonistic toward you because of your commitment to integrity and purity. But without exception, light exposes darkness. If your husband is walking in darkness, walking in the light may cause him to blink or be defensive. But persevere. God tells us that the best way to win our husbands is through our actions, not our words (1 Peter 3:1–2).

### Use Esther's example of timing and tact.

Sometimes it's important to be very upfront with your husband when changes need to be made. Early in their marriage, Martin Luther's wife watched him battle bouts of depression, even question God's willingness or ability to help him through a difficult trial. Without saying a word, she donned a black dress and veil, reserved for times of mourning.

When Luther asked why she was dressed that way, she commented, "Because God is dead. It's obvious by the way you're acting." [2]

I'd call that the direct approach!

There may be times when you'll need to be forceful and even confrontational with your husband. Yet when it comes to encouraging him to behave in God-honoring ways, you would do well to study the life of Esther.

Esther was a beautiful Jewish queen who saved her countrymen and herself from an unfair death sentence by using courage, timing, and tact. The book of Esther tells her story, and if you don't know it, I encourage you to read it for yourself.

Many of the ways Esther treated her husband, the king, were unique to that time, but you can learn from her wisdom in looking for the right time and setting to talk with your husband about what you hope will change.

The first time Esther came to her husband unannounced, it was with great fear because according to the custom of the day, he could have had her killed for approaching him uninvited. But when he responded receptively, she used great tact and discernment in talking to him about the Jews' life-and-death predicament.

Like Esther, we should be students of our husbands when we approach them on an issue or problem. Raising our voices or badgering them won't bring about change. Understanding when our husbands are most approachable, and talking to them in an honoring way, will help to lower their initial defenses.

For example, if your husband isn't a night owl, don't try to engage him just as he's getting into bed. If he spends much of his time working over lunch or dinner, schedule a dinner date at a secluded table in a restaurant and talk with him there about your concern. Being a student of your husband, like Esther was, can go a long way toward resolving concerns successfully. And remember, Esther may have used tact and timing, but she still had the courage to confront her husband over what she thought was terribly wrong.

### Encourage accountability as an individual and as a couple.

Without a doubt, one of the best tools for encouraging purity in your marriage and family is *loving accountability*. It's a concept John and I are committed to. Over our sixteen years of marriage, we've been in couples' groups, Bible study groups, men's and women's accountability groups, and one-on-one discipleship teams. While the groups and formats have changed over the years, the encouragement we've received from loving friends has remained powerful.

I can't encourage you enough to make yourselves accountable to another couple, a special friend or two, or a small group. You might consider teaching a Sunday school class where others will watch your example, giving you something to live up to. When we let others get close to us, they can help us keep our faith, attitudes, and actions God-honoring and pure. Trying to make it on our own not only quarrels with biblical wisdom, but sets us up for isolation and temptation. It's been said of isolated Christians, "The wolf loves lone sheep."

I challenge you and your husband to walk the walk and talk the talk—along with some loving friends who can encourage you to stay committed to purity—and experience God's blessing as a result.

### Notes

[1] J.D. Douglas, *The New Bible Dictionary*, (Grand Rapids, Mich.: Wm. B. Eerdmans Publishing Company, August, 1971), 1066.

[2] Unpublished class notes from Dr. John Hannah, Church History 201, Dallas Theological Seminary, 1976.

[3] James Strong, *Strong's Exhaustive Concordance* (Grand Rapids, Mich.: Baker Book House), 819-820.

**Cindy Trent** is the co-author of *How to Be Your Husband's Best Friend* (Piñon Press, 1995). A former elementary teacher, she earned her bachelor's degree from the University of Arizona and her master's degree in early childhood education from Texas Woman's University. She and her husband, John, have two daughters.

## Questions for Discussion

1. Of the five marks of purity described in this chapter, which one is the most difficult for you to emulate? For your husband? Do any of these characteristics seem beyond reach for either of you? Why or why not?

2. Describe a time when you or your husband clung to your ethical standards or stood up for Christ at great risk to your career or relationships. Describe a time when you or your husband compromised your standards or your witness. What were the professional, social, emotional, or spiritual results in both cases?

3. Is there anyone against whom you are holding a grudge? How can you move toward forgiveness? Why do you think forgiveness is an important attitude to practice?

4. Describe some ways you encouraged a commitment to purity in your home this past week. What are some specific ways you could encourage your husband to develop the five marks of purity in the week ahead?

5. To whom are you and your husband accountable to others on the issues of purity discussed in this chapter? If you do not have relationships in which you practice loving accountability, with whom might you develop some? What action will you take to establish such relationships?

# CHAPTER SEVEN

# Building a Strong Marriage

### LINDA WEBER

*A* happy marriage doesn't just happen. It takes a lot of work. I know that from experience.

As the eldest child in each of our families, my husband Stu and I are both strong-willed and we've had to work at overcoming challenges in our marriage. We didn't automatically know how to have a strong marriage; we've had to learn how to have one. We've sought to know God's plan as we've prayed daily and talked with wise counselors. Proverbs 11:14 says, "For lack of guidance a nation falls, but many advisers make victory sure." I pray that you are open to the guidance of wise counsel.

Christian marriages today are going downstream in a fast-moving current. We're about to drift over the edge, and we don't even know it. Like the frog who boiled to death ever so slowly, unaware of the change of temperature, we have become numb to the destructive patterns that surround us.

We can't allow ourselves to be swept away. If couples are going to learn to swim against the tide, there's a lot of learning to be done. This chapter is designed to give some hands-on help on how you can aid your husband in building a strong marriage. When you encourage your man so that he feels your desire for oneness, your marriage will be stronger and the motivation for developing a strong family will be strengthened as well.

As a wife, you are key to motivating your husband in these areas. I was reminded of this recently when, after working at home all day, I received a call from Stu. He, too, had been working all day and had had several intense meetings. He'd called at the end of his sessions to see how I was, as he knew I was under pressure. He asked if I would mind if he made a quick stop on the way home to check on his parents (now in their seventies). Even though I was tired and wanted to unload my frustrations, I encouraged him to do what he needed to and said I was looking forward to seeing him when he got home.

Later that evening he thanked me for my upbeat attitude and for supporting his choice to visit his parents. He told me that when he'd called, he was exhausted and was unsure of how my demanding day would have affected me. When he detected in my voice that inviting safe place that home provided, he greatly anticipated coming home.

I'm glad I made that choice that evening. I don't always. I saw once again how great my influence is in motivating and energizing my husband. You have the same influence in your marriage. How can *you* support and encourage your husband to build a strong marriage?

## Know Your Man

Before you can support and encourage your husband, you need to know him. You need to know what tickles him, what makes him tick, and what ticks him off.

Learn about his masculinity. When a man is encouraged to be the man he was intended to be, everybody wins. He soars with confidence, his wife's needs are fulfilled, and his children's hopes are realized. In *Tender Warrior*, my husband, Stu, says that God's intention for a man is that he always be an initiator, but never a tyrant...always a provider and protector, but never a brute...always a mentor and model, but never a know-it-all...always a friend and lover, but never a smotherer.[1]

As we support God's plan rather than try to force our husbands into our mold, they truly become what we are longing to have. We do ourselves a big favor when we become a student of the differences between men and women.

Encourage your husband to pursue relationships or activities that develop his masculinity. For example, men need strong friendships with other men. In his book *Locking Arms*, Stu talks about how he suspects that David's relationship with Bathsheba would never have flourished if David had had an accountable relationship with Jonathan at the time.[2] According to my husband, men need other men to encourage their growth and accountability. As wives, we would be wise to invite such friendships rather than resent the time our husbands spend away from us.

If your husband has a friendship with someone who is a negative influence in his life, you should tactfully speak up about his choice of friends. Instead of condemning his actions and thereby raising his defenses, ask him questions about his friends. When you precede these talks with prayer, God will help you discern the questions that will help reveal these men's character and in turn show your husband what kind of behavior the relationships are producing. As he hears himself talk, he may realize that his behavior is destructive both to himself and to your relationship.

Give your husband the freedom to pursue recreation with other men. Whatever his passion is—hunting, fishing, golf, carpentry, cycling—let him enjoy it in the company of other guys. Stu and I have three sons, so I'm the only female in our house. I've had to remind myself that they need time together without me so they can enjoy activities that have more masculine appeal. It takes conscious awareness on my part not to have a pity party.

## Do Everything You Can to Enhance Your Sex Life

One of the best ways to a man's heart is through meeting his sexual needs. Whether you meet him at the door in Saran wrap (remember *The Total Woman?*) or find your own ways to be creatively tantalizing, expend some energy on meeting the needs God has instilled in him. Sex is usually a much more powerful force in our man's life than in ours. Don't minimize its importance.

The Bible clearly states that we are to enjoy sex with our spouse. Proverbs 5 advises men to avoid the seductions of an adulteress whose speech is smoother than oil (v. 3), and instead, "Drink water from your own cistern, running water from your own well.... Let them be yours alone, never to be shared with strangers. May your fountain be blessed, and may you rejoice in the wife of your youth.... May her breasts satisfy you always, may you ever be captivated by her love" (v. 15-19).

Wives should heed this admonition. The entire Song of

Songs describes the pleasures of a physical relationship between a man and a woman. Are we listening? Where did some Christians ever get the idea that sex was intended for procreation only? Our husbands are waiting for us and they need our sexual attention—frequently. God made them that way, and He designed our incredible differences to blend together and compliment one another.

As you increase your awareness of the differences between men and women, you will be able to pursue your husband with greater skill. Let your body satisfy him and learn to thoroughly enjoy him. Think about pleasing him. Try variety. One of the best ways to keep your husband from being tempted to go elsewhere is to keep the chemistry burning between you. A strong offense keeps you from being put on the defense. Be smart up-front.

Since men are visual, we can support our husbands by paying attention to what they see when they look at us. Yes, we could respond to this by arguing, "What about him and his responsibilities? It's what's on the inside that matters anyway." While this is true, it's also true that taking active responsibility can also be right and true before God. People throughout time have shunned personal responsibility, but I've found that my life is much more effective if I concentrate on what I can do rather than focus on my disappointments or another person's responsibilities.

Ask yourself, *What have I done to keep fit and be attractive? Do I care how I ring his bell and bring him running, even years after I won his heart?* Consider whether exercise should be a part of your formula. It helps to decrease lethargy and can increase your ability to be tuned into and alive for your man.

You will be a better lover if you learn to discipline your mind when making love with your husband. During lovemaking, does your mind ever start wandering? Do you think, *Oh shoot, I forgot to stir the Jell-O and now my dish won't be ready in time for company.... I wonder what I should fix for dinner tomorrow when our friends come over.... I wonder if the kids can hear this bed squeaking...?* Because it's natural for a woman's antennas to be up and out at all times, we're aware of what's happening or what needs to happen. Unfortunately, this means that during love-making our thoughts can be elsewhere if we're not working at disciplining our minds. If we're not mentally present, our husbands will know it and get a message that we aren't interested.

As wives, we need to be aware that we have this tendency to split our attention among many things. Then, we need to work hard to concentrate on our husbands and what we can do to be all we can be for that moment and always.

## Have Fun Together

You will enjoy your marriage more if you laugh a lot together. Try to find ways to experience pleasure that endears you to each other. Enjoy fun little names for each other that mean something special just to the two of you. Develop secrets together, private jokes that keep you whispering fun nothings and keep you intrigued with each other. Wink at him and watch him melt. He'll love it.

Schedule time to go out and do something fun, even if your budget is tight. Be creative. Find ways to make fun happen. Instead of thinking, *Oh we can't do that!* find a way; be persistent and watch your dreams come true.

My friend Lisa has learned how to do this on a shoestring budget. She read Mike Yorkey's book, *Saving Money Any Way You Can*,[3] which offered her lots of ways to save money on a daily basis, even on necessities like groceries, housing, and cars. The money she saved on these things allowed her to feel more free to set aside some of their budget for fun times. Lisa realized that living on a tight budget can cause a lot of stress on a marriage, so she wisely made sure that she and her husband didn't sacrifice spontaneity and fun.

Another way to have fun is to make memories together. Find enjoyable things to do and then record them in photos. Display these photos in frames around your home or office. The reminder of your special times together help endear you to each other and stimulate you to make more memories.

As you plan, think *togetherness* rather than independence. Plan events you can anticipate together. Show interest in his world and what he does and enjoys. During a recent sabbatical Stu went on a trip to his birthplace which he had not seen in many years. He needed a little time away to enjoy reflecting on a lot of things that are important to him. That may not sound like entering his world, but because I was happy for him to have this time away, he knew that I cared what was important to him. In his frequent calls home, he was bubbling to share with me the fun of seeing this or doing that or just remembering good times. I loved getting excited with him, and I was glad that he wanted to share his feelings with me. It was my privilege to enter his world by being interested and showing my pleasure for him. It was good for us.

## Love Him Unconditionally

Loving your husband unconditionally means loving him even if he doesn't change or perform as you'd like. This is God's way of loving. Does it come naturally to any of us? No. We are born self-centered. We think, *What about me and what I want?*

When I speak with other women about this, I typically hear, "But you don't know my husband!" But loving unconditionally means loving someone despite his behavior. How many times have you refused to accept your husband because he hasn't lived up to your expectations? Maybe he doesn't fix things around the house that have been broken for months, even years. Maybe he stays at work and doesn't participate in household duties that are weighing you down. He might forget things that are important to you. Or perhaps he spends money foolishly or has his priorities out of order. (Your order? We often see things differently from our husbands.)

As Christian women, you and I get to choose whether we will put others first and accept the responsibility of doing what's right, or accuse and condemn our husbands. Being unselfish means loving with acceptance, regardless of his performance. Does your husband feel in his bones that you love him the way he is now, or does he sense that you're waiting for something to change before you cherish him unconditionally?

## Be Supportive

Does your spirit motivate your husband to be a true leader in your marriage? John Piper helps us understand God's intention for male-female relationships in his book, *What's the Difference*. He says, "The Biblical reality of a wife's submission would take different forms depending on the quality of a husband's leadership. This can be seen best if we define submission not in terms of specific behaviors, but as a *disposition* to yield to the husband's authority and an inclination to his leadership...." [4]

Ask yourself if your daily choices demonstrate that you desire to go forward *together* as a couple, or if they indicate that you are following an independent course. When your husband is grumpy and cantankerous or depressed, following his lead can be a challenge. Rise to the occasion with all your creativity and intelligence. Be determined not to give up on winning his heart when your first attempts go awry. Successful people never give up. Successful marriages are built on commitment and perseverance.

If women will commit themselves to practicing biblical, true submission, they will build strength throughout generations to come. Consider the words of Richard Strauss:

> When Dad abdicates his position of authority in the home, Mom usually assumes the role she was never intended to have. The unhappy combination of a disinterested father and an overbearing mother can drive children to run away from home, enter early and unwise marriages, or suffer emotional difficulties and personality deficiencies. Dad must take the lead.... A dominant wife and mother confuses the children.... If mothers and fathers have equal authority, the child does not know which one to obey. He will use the one against the other to get his own way, and will soon lose respect for one or both parents. Studies have shown that children with conduct problems often have domineering, high-strung mothers. But if a child knows beyond all doubt that Dad is the head of the house, that Mom speaks for Dad, and that Dad's authority backs up what she says, he will be more apt to obey and will have more love and respect for both his parents.[5]

In this day and age of blatant domestic abuse, I must add a note of caution: biblical support and submission does *not* mean accepting abuse. Any woman who is living in a physically abusive marriage must pursue help. Do not enable destructive behavior. Consider consulting James Dobson's book, *Love Must Be Tough*, for guidelines.[6]

## Create a Positive Feeling in His Heart

Physical expressions of affection can touch a man's heart more than anything. Those gentle touches, along with a smile and look of admiration, have an impact. So does the sight of good food when he's tired and hungry.

Positively reinforce your husband regularly. When he's feeling good about himself, he will more likely feel good about you. Praise him in front of your children. Talk him up to the children. Tell others how you appreciate your husband.

Ask questions about how he's feeling and then listen to his answers. Share your own heart's concerns so you develop intimacy. Passivity simply sets you up to experience emotional walls in your relationship. No one can guess what's going on in another person's head. Be assertive about sharing feelings in a non-threatening manner. Instead of pointing an accusing finger when he doesn't follow through on something he said he'd do, say, "I am feeling disappointed." This kind of honest statement is a lot more inviting than complaining, "You blew it! You never do what you say you'll do!"

Show your husband that he pleases you. No doubt you can think of his numerous shortcomings and how you'd like to see him change, but if you'll just accept him with a smile, you'll do both of you a favor. He can literally come alive from your praise and acceptance and renew all those positive feelings you once had.

## Actively Promote Communication

Promoting communication is part of relational mainte-nance. We cannot expect a relationship to stay strong if we deprive it of nourishment. In fact, we can cause it to suffocate if we don't keep the channels of communication open.

Knowing how to foster communication in marriage and families is critical, yet many people are ignorant of the neces-sary skills. Few of us take classes in high school or college on improving communication, yet we communicate every day. We would be wise to cultivate good communication skills before the misunderstandings in our relationships have practi-cally destroyed us.

Your attitude and approach toward your husband can either promote or discourage further interaction and communica-tion. When I talk with Stu about concerns that are important to me, I try to remember that he'll hear me better if I do so in a safe and positive atmosphere. If I help him feel good about himself through my positive demeanor, we set a more friendly, compatible context in which to discuss some issue that needs our attention.

Whether or not you feel that you need help with commu-nication, I recommend that you attend something like the FamilyLife marriage or parenting conference to boost your skills. For more information about these seminars, write or call for a free conference brochure:

FamilyLife
3900 North Rodney Parham
Little Rock, AR 72212
1-800-FL-TODAY (1-800-358-6329)

### Show Him Respect

It's a biblical mandate. Ephesians 5:33 says, "...the wife must respect her husband." The Amplified Bible translates, "...let the wife see that she respects and reverences her husband—that she notices him, regards him, honors him, prefers him, venerates and esteems him; and that she defers to him, praises him, and loves and admires him exceedingly."

We honor God as we fulfill His command to respect the man He has given us throughout all the seasons of our marriage, be they good, bad, or ugly. So, build up your husband. Be the one who makes him feel like a million bucks. His ego needs it, and both of you will profit more than you can imagine. Try it.

If you feel resistant to this idea, you might consider why. Is it selfishness on your part? Maybe his choices in life don't seem to merit your respect. If so, remember that God doesn't hold you responsible for your husband's choices but for respecting him as a person. I encourage you to step out in faith and tell your man how wonderful he is. Find the positive. Compliment him repeatedly. You may have to call a rescue squad to pick him up off the floor, but you'll certainly be a winner in this pursuit of showing honor.

The Bible tells us that women can win their husbands without a word. 1 Peter 3:1–2 says, "Wives, in the same way be submissive to your husbands so that, if any of them do not believe the word, they may be won over without words by the behavior of their wives, when they see the purity and reverence of your lives."

Wow! What an opportunity we have to influence our husbands for the Kingdom! We also have a responsibility to behave in ways that can win them over. Stop and let this concept sink in so you can take more concrete steps to activate it in your life. Ask yourself, *Am I good at this? How can I show my husband respect? What can I genuinely compliment him for?*

Your husband needs to feel that you respect his leadership. Be alert to ways you can influence him, but let him take the lead. Even if something was your idea, he'll feel good about being able to proceed as you enthusiastically follow and praise him for each step he takes. Let him feel good about being a leader. Don't give in to the temptation to take over, even if you are more capable in a certain area.

In our house, I keep the financial books. This was a decision we made together because I enjoy the job more than Stu does. But our marriage in general is under Stu's leadership. We both give input on decisions, but the final say—and responsibility—rests with him.

Part of respecting your man's leadership is trying *not* to be his mother. You are not his conscience; you are the person who can point him to higher ground by demonstrating respect for his leadership, publicly and privately.

## Be Aware of the Unique Stressors in Your Lives

Keep your eyes open so you're always aware of ways to maintain and improve your marriage. Left unattended, what God has joined together may fall apart. You'll need to build fortress-like walls around weak areas so your relationship doesn't crumble.

First, be aware of the family of origin each of you came from and what frame of reference you each bring to life every day. Experts tell us that we live out as adults what we learned at home as children. For example, do either of you come from a strong conservative background? As a result of those years of restraint, could either of you be harboring some unconscious desires for "freedom"?

Also be aware of the potential for relational chemistry—that is, to the dynamics that can develop between men and women, specifically your husband and other women. Lack of awareness causes many Christian marriages to be threatened.

Listen carefully to Dennis Rainey's instruction to Christians:

> High school chemistry taught me a very valuable lesson. When certain substances come into close contact, they can form a chemical reaction. I proved that one day during my senior year of high school when I dropped a jar full of pure sodium off a bridge into a river and nearly blew up the bridge. You'd think that I would have at least had enough sense to have stepped off the bridge!
>
> What I've learned since then is that many people don't respect the laws of chemistry any more than I did back then. They mix volatile ingredients without giving much thought to the explosion which could occur. I've discovered that many married people don't understand that a chemical reaction can occur with someone other than their mates. Don't misunderstand me here—I'm not just talking about sexual attraction; I'm referring to a reaction of two hearts, the chemistry of two souls.
>
> This is emotional adultery—an intimacy with the opposite sex outside the marriage. Emotional adultery is unfaithfulness of the

heart. When two people begin talking of intimate struggles, doubts or feelings, they may be
sharing their souls in a way that God intended
exclusively for the marriage relationship.
Emotional adultery is friendship with the
opposite sex that has progressed too far.

Often it begins as a casual relationship at
work, school, even church. A husband talks
with a female co-worker over coffee and shares
some struggles he's facing with his wife or kids.
She tells of similar problems, and soon the
emotions ricochet so rapidly that their hearts
ignite and can ultimately become fused together as one. To those who've experienced it, this
catalytic bonding seems too real to deny.[7]

As you work to guard your marriage, I recommend that you
read *The Snare* by Lois Mowday Rabey.[8] She helps her readers
understand the emotional and sexual entanglements that are
subtly but powerfully overtaking many good but inappropriately
involved people.

You need to educate yourself about human tendencies during various seasons of life. Some behaviors are predictable, and
being aware of them can help you prevent trouble. Recognize
your personal responsibility and exercise it. You can't be
responsible for your husband's choices, but your own actions
can strongly encourage specific behavior in him, positively or
negatively.

When working through some of these issues, professional
counseling is often useful. Don't be afraid to seek help. In the
process, remember that things usually have to get worse

before they get better. You can make it!

### Make Sure He Has Reason to Admire You.

Do you have qualities that naturally draw him to you? Which list below most accurately describes you? And how many negative traits are you willing to work at changing?

| Negative | Positive |
| --- | --- |
| Selfishly oriented | Unselfishly oriented |
| Distant/aloof | Able to be intimate |
| Demanding | Giving |
| Doubting | Trusting |
| Confused | Wise |
| Wavering | Loyal |
| Deceptive | Possess integrity |
| Avoids responsibility | Takes Responsibility |
| Complainer | Joyful |
| Exaggerating | Truthful |
| Impatient | Patient |
| Threatened | Teachable |
| Assuming | Grateful |
| Explosive | Peaceful |
| Rigid | Flexible |
| Driven | Balanced |
| Destructive | Nurturing |

As you look at the positive list, which qualities first attracted him to you? Do those qualities still characterize you? It takes work to cultivate a positive outlook and behavior. Are you willing to invest the effort?

## The Legacy of a Strong Marriage

When you work hard to develop depth in your marriage, you are prepared to offer your children the gift they need most: a model for their future.

Confident children don't just materialize. That twenty-year window of nurturing and modeling lends you a great opportunity to shape lives for generations to come. You are building a legacy. When you recognize the thousands of things you do at home as messages you're sending your children about their importance and value, you can feel honored. You're not wasting your time; you're helping the next generation become solid citizens in a society that lacks purpose and direction. What a role you have to play!

As you seek to warm the hearts in your home by encouraging your husband and helping to build a strong marriage, you will enjoy his pleasure and have assurance that you've provided your children with a rich heritage. God's character is reflected and His reputation can shine. Everybody wins.

### Notes

[1]Stu Weber, *Tender Warrior*, (Sisters, Or.: Multnomah Books, 1993), p.35ff.

[2]Stu Weber, *Locking Arms*, (Sisters, Or.: Multnomah Books, 1995), p.155-156.

[3]Mike Yorkey, *Saving Money Any Way You Can*, (Ann Arbor, Mich.: Servant Publications, 1994).

[4]John Piper, *What's the Difference?* (Westchester, Ill.: Crossway Books, 1990), p.37.

[5]Richard L. Strauss, *How to Raise Confident Children*, (Grand Rapids, Mich.: Baker, 1975), p.120, 131.

[6]James Dobson, *Love Must be Tough*, (Dallas, Tex.: Word, 1983).

[7]Dennis Rainey, *My Soapbox*, newsletter for Family Ministry, October 10, 1988, p.1

[8]Lois Mowday Rabey, *The Snare*, (Colorado Springs: Navpress, 1988).

**Linda Weber** is a conference speaker and the author of the best-selling book, *Mom, You're Incredible* (Focus on the Family, 1994). She is married to Stu (pastor, conference speaker, and best-selling author). Both Stu and Linda are national speakers for FamilyLife conferences. They live in Gresham, Oregon, and are the parents of three sons—Kent, Blake, and Ryan.

## Questions for Discussion

1. Do you agree that, as a wife, you are key to motivating your husband to build a strong marriage and family? Why or why not? Give a recent example of a time when you used your influence to motivate and energize your husband.

2. Of the ten ways to encourage your husband described in this chapter, which one(s) do you need the most improvement in? Describe a time when you used one of these ten tools well, as well as a time when you failed to use one. What were the results in both situations?

3. Is there something in your husband's life that you're waiting for him to change? Does he sense this? How would it look for you to practice loving him unconditionally in this area?

4. Can you think of a time when you motivated your husband to make positive changes in his life without speaking a word (1 Peter 3:1-2)? Describe it.

5. What qualities does your husband most admire in you What qualities do you think he wishes you'd develop? What are some specific ways you can build these positive qualities within yourself in the month ahead?

# CHAPTER EIGHT

# Honoring Your Church and Pastor

### DARCY KIMMEL

As the dark clouds rolled in and the cold wind picked up, Jim felt a knot form in his stomach. He was going to have to work quickly to secure the sheep safely in their pen before the full force of the storm hit and darkness covered the hills.

"Ninety-six, ninety-seven, ninety-eight…." *Wouldn't you know it! Those same two sheep had wandered off again.* Jim had half a mind to just let them fend for themselves, but he didn't have that luxury. They weren't his sheep. He had taken an oath before their owner that he would do all he could to keep them safe and cared for.

Fastening the latch on the sheep fold, he whispered a prayer for the protection of the ninety-eight and then turned to face the forest that was quickly succumbing to the shadows of the storm. Cold. Fear. Fatigue. He felt all three as he buttoned his coat tightly and pulled his hat down over his ears. *It's going to be a long night.*

Leaning into the wind, his eyes fell on the village lights below. *I hope Mary isn't worried about me being late. She's more patient with me than I deserve. I was supposed to restock the wood pile tonight. It's so cold, and Jimmy was running a fever when I left this morning. Dear God, don't let her try to chop the wood herself. I couldn't bear it if anything happened to her or the baby growing inside of her.*

The shrill wind and the sleeting rain was going to make it difficult to hear the bleating of the wayward sheep. Funny, though, how Jim could hear his own stomach growling from hunger and his teeth chattering from the cold. Trimming his lantern and holding it out in front of him, he began to retrace the path he had led the sheep over earlier that day. And as he moved deeper into the woods, he prayed that his commitment to his sheep would not succumb to the growing desire within him to give up.

Two hours and several exhausting miles later he heard something that made him think he was dreaming. *What was that? It sounds like... no, it couldn't be.* For a second he thought the wind was calling his name. *Boy, I'm more exhausted than I realized.* But wait, there were lights coming over the hill— five, maybe more. Then he heard his name again and began to see men attached to the floating lanterns.

"Jim! Hey, Jim, there you are." As the group came closer, he saw they were his neighbors. One of them continued, "We knew you'd been up here tending to your sheep. When we saw the storm, we thought we'd better check to see if you'd made it home. Mary was nervous, but she figured you were probably having to search for some strays. She knew you wouldn't be able to come home until you found them. The fire was low so we replenished the wood supply. Don't worry

about Jimmy, he's been taking his medicine and his temperature is almost down to normal. Mary said you hadn't eaten
since lunch, so she sent you a sandwich and hot coffee. Why
don't you sit down and eat. We'll find the sheep."

This lantern brigade is the answer to every pastor's prayer.
Many pastors are over-burdened by time demands, exhausted
from the effects of sin in the congregation, beaten down by
their insecurities, worried about their own families, and
forced to do the work of many. As football coach Bill
McCartney said, "They're overworked, under-compensated,
under-appreciated, beleaguered, and exasperated."[1]

God's servants have paid a high price to follow orders. But
it doesn't have to be this way. Just as Aaron and Hur secured
the victory by holding up Moses' arms, our husbands and our
families can hold up the arms of the pastors in our local
church and join in the sacred mission that God intends to
accomplish through His Church.

In this chapter, we will learn how we can encourage our
husbands to be faithful lantern bearers—men who can be
counted on to uphold God's work and God's workers.

## Getting Some Perspective

As a pastor steps up to the pulpit every Sunday and looks at
his congregation, he realizes that although he knows intimate
details of many of these people, there are very few that he can
call friends. He will attend weddings, baptisms, graduations,

and ball games for them. He will be by their bedside and graveside, but very few of them will be at his side for him and his family.

As he thinks about this, he doesn't spend his time complaining or feeling sorry for himself. He accepts that this just goes with the job description. He was warned about it in seminary. He just didn't realize that it would feel this lonely.

When God places his hand on a man and sets him aside for ministry, it is not an invitation to enlist. Rather, it is a holy calling, a divine draft. This Christian soldier realizes that God's work on earth through His church is a major part of His eternal plan. In Matthew 16:18, Christ says that "...on this rock I will build my church, and the gates of Hades will not overcome it." Based on this verse, we can be sure that the church is here to stay. And if we're serious about being a part of God's work on earth, then we need to join forces with our pastor and local church.

If we desire to encourage and support our husbands as they commit to praying for our pastor and giving to the church their time and resources, then we must make the same promise to them as the head shepherds of our families. We must support them, honor them, pray for them, and give of ourselves to them. A husband is more equipped to carry out these commitments to his pastor and church when he feels the same commitments from his wife. She is his partner in life, love, and ministry.

## Supporting the Mission

Only two institutions take you from the cradle to the grave: the church and the family. They are both primary threads in the tapestry of life. Because the two are so interwoven, it is imperative that a wife embrace this commitment together with her husband.

Do you know what the mission of your church is? It's hard to catch the vision if you don't know what it is. Most churches have distilled their purposes into a "mission statement." If you don't know what this is, call the church office and ask. Then write it out and give a copy to your husband.

If your church does not have a formal mission statement, then look at the one God gives all of us in 1 Peter 2:9–10: "But you are a chosen people, a royal priesthood, a holy nation, a people belonging to God, that you may declare the praises of him who called you out of darkness into his wonderful light. Once you were not a people, but now you are the people of God; once you had not received mercy, but now you have received mercy."

When the mission is clear, your family will be better prepared to join the cause.

One of the greatest gifts a husband and wife can bring to a church is a healthy marriage and family. Granted, all families have needs, and we all depend on our church to help us meet those needs sometimes. But the fewer problems we have, the less personal attention we require from the church and the more we can give.

Healthy marriages and families do not materialize on their own. They require a lot of hard work, commitment, and prayer. Attend a marriage seminar, brush up on your communication skills, eat dinner together as a family. Counteract the attacks of culture and present the pew with a happy, healthy family unit.

The reputation of your church in the community is only as good as that of its members. Never do anything to shame the name of your fellowship. Our actions and our words must be above reproach as we deal with our neighbors and business associates.

When we view the church as an asset to our family and see our family as strategic to the mission of our church, then we see ourselves as partners in ministry. We take ownership. We're a team. The church becomes our church; its ministry becomes our mission.

## Honoring Your Pastor

Scripture teaches that we are to respect and hold in highest regard those who are the shepherds. It might help to know that we are asked to do this not because of who our pastor is, or because of his training or abilities, but because of the work he has been called to do. "Now we ask you, brothers, to respect those who work hard among you, who are over you in the Lord and who admonish you. Hold them in the highest regard in love because of their work. Live in peace with each other" (1 Thessalonians 5:12–13).

A pastor should be honored because he has been placed in a position of leadership by God. God uses mere men to do His work here on earth. Our honor for our pastor must be based on his ordained position in our church. When a couple real- izes the unique demands and unmet needs of their pastor, they will become aware of how to honor him.

### Appreciate His Work.

If any of us could walk a day in the shoes of our pastor, we would be much more appreciative of his work. One way to show appreciation is to speak well of him. Too many pastors are not only roasted at Sunday lunch, but are charbroiled, filleted, and fried. When people go to church in a *what's in it for me* frame of mind, they misuse and squander the opportunity to worship. Our children mimic our dislikes and prejudices. If we want to contribute a healthy family to our church, then our children must be taught how to honor their pastor. As wives, we should never pass on gossip or let someone say something unkind without admonishing them to refrain.

All the pastors I interviewed for this chapter mentioned how important words of encouragement were to them. Handshakes and pats on the back after the sermon are great. Even better, because it shows an extra effort, is a note specifically thanking your pastor for a godly action or character trait, or a life-changing teaching.

Dr. Bill Brewer, a friend and pastor in Richardson, Texas, told me about Pastor Appreciation Month at their church. During this time, the pastors in his church received hundreds of notes and their wives and families got almost as many. To make expressing appreciation easy, a tree was placed in the foyer of the church with a table and note cards next to it. People were able to write a note on the spot and attach it to the "tree of appreciation." Some of these notes even contained gifts of appreciation.

Another long-time friend and pastor, Rick Efird, told me that his congregation is sending their entire pastoral staff to the Promise Keepers pastor's conference. All expenses are being paid for by individual gifts of money and frequent flyer miles. An investment in your pastor and in his family is an investment in a kingdom where God pays incredible dividends.

My own pastor, Darryl DelHousaye, said that he feels honored when someone else takes the initiative. Most people expect and assume that the pastor should initiate friendships, prayer times, ministry projects, and service. Darryl says when someone shows interest in him or his family or in his vision for ministry and volunteers to take action instead of waiting to be asked, he feels valued and esteemed.

Occasionally I talk with someone who is church shopping. If they've been at it for a long time, there will likely be two problems. Either their expectations are so high that even Jesus and the heavenly host would not fit the bill, or they are merely looking for what they can get out of the church rather than looking for a ministry they can put themselves into. We must deal with our pastor and our church with grace. Pastors are not perfect. Churches are not perfect. People are not perfect. When a pastor is allowed to be himself, be vulnerable, and make honest mistakes, then he feels honored.

### Grow from His Instruction.

I've said it many times and so have you: "What's the use?" We iron and starch our daughter's 100 percent cotton dress, curl and fix her hair for a party, and then she goes outside and plays soccer with the boys. A pastor feels the same way when Sunday after Sunday he teaches how God says we ought to live, only to have many in his congregation go do the exact opposite.

All the pastors I spoke with said they felt honored when their people valued their instruction enough to act upon it. Dr. Robert Lewis, who pastors in Little Rock, Arkansas, says he is honored "when men are captured by a vision of using their gifts for a kingdom cause, whether it is inside or outside of the church community."

If your husband is not part of a small accountability group or men's Bible study, do everything you can to make it easy for him to go. Without being a nag, find out when these groups meet and write down the schedule for him. If it costs a few bucks for him to meet at a restaurant, then don't begrudge that eternal investment. Let him tell you what he's learning without criticizing him in the areas in which he falls short. Don't take on the role of the Holy Spirit in his life and attempt to plot out a plan for his journey to spiritual maturity. Just be glad he's involved in the group and make it as uncomplicated as possible for him to participate.

When a pastor sees that his efforts are making a difference in the lives of his flock, he feels honored. The Apostle John reflects the sentiments of many pastors: "I have no greater joy than to hear that my children are walking in the truth" (3 John 1:4).

### Pray for His Work.

A shepherd needs spiritual wisdom and understanding to guide, feed, and protect his flock. Every day he is called upon to help make decisions that change people's destiny. They want to know: Should we get married? Can we get divorced? Why can't we have a baby? Why can't we save our baby? What college should we attend? What job should we take? What do I do next? What do I do now? Answering these questions requires divine wisdom.

Pastors are only human. They, like the rest of us, may make mistakes. Unfortunately and unfairly, the mistakes they make can be devastating. A pastor is only a whisper away from destruction and our pastors desperately need us to cover them in prayer as they dodge the onslaught of the enemy. Satan is after the shepherds. He knows that if he can destroy the shepherd, the sheep will self-destruct.

Lift your shepherd up in prayer. Replace critical pettiness with powerful petitions. Your family has a lot at stake. Your congregation has a lot to gain.

Pastors travel through the valley of the shadow of death over and over again with their flock. In the midst of their own heartaches they are called upon to give comfort, to offer answers, to make sense. But often they're just getting into their car at the cemetery when their car phone alerts them to a call from another needy parishioner. Pastors need prayer for endurance, resilience, and refreshment. They need supernatural strength to bear the burdens of many.

If you would like to write down a prayer that your family could pray for your pastor every day, I would suggest the one in Colossians 1:9–12: "For this reason, since the day we heard about you, we have not stopped praying for you and asking God to fill you with the knowledge of his will through all spiritual wisdom and understanding. And we pray this in order that you may live a life worthy of the Lord and may please him in every way: bearing fruit in every good work, growing in the knowledge of God, being strengthened with all power according to his glorious might so that you may have great endurance and patience, and joyfully giving thanks to the Father, who has qualified you to share in the inheritance of the saints in the kingdom of light."

### Pray for His Family.

I went to a Christian liberal arts college. Enrolled at Bryan College were a lot of PKs and MKs: preachers' and missionaries' kids. Sometimes these were among the most rebellious and unhappy students on campus. Some were bitter about unavailable parents, unfinanced hopes, unreasonable demands, and unrealized dreams.

We need to pray for our pastor and his family. Pray that he will be able to be the father he knows he should be. Pray that his family can have large quantities of quality time together. Pray for their health. Pray for their marriage. Pray for the salvation of their children. After all, your pastor prays those prayers for you and your family.

Someone shared a simple prayer strategy with me many years ago, and I have passed it on to others. As I go through my day performing servant tasks for my family, rather than grumble, I pray. As I iron Tim's shirts, I petition God for him. As I wade through Karis's room, I intercede on her behalf. As I brush the tangles from Shiloh's long blonde hair, I pray for her. As I pick up Cody's hat for the fiftieth time, I make supplication for him. And as I try to match up Colt's clean socks, I lift him up to the Lord.

Constant reminders in my home encourage me to pray for my family. Why not do the same for your pastor? Put a photo of his family on your refrigerator. Put their name on the bookmark in your Bible. Designate Sunday morning grace as a time to pray for your pastor and your church. James 5:16 promises that "the prayer of a righteous man (woman) is powerful and effective."

### Pray for His Christian Walk.

In the midst of pointing his congregation down the right paths, a pastor must also guard his own walk. As I talked with my pastor friends about this area of prayer, they freely shared some things they wish the people in their congregation would pray for:

- a balanced life
- moral purity
- devotion to Christ
- focused obedience
- accountability
- strength to say yes
- courage to say no
- soulmates
- simplicity
- protection from the enemy
- a life without regret

These are the earnest requests of men who are serious about finishing the race and finishing well.

If this kind of prayer isn't already happening in your church, then petition and encourage your husband to start up or become a member of a prayer team. Bill Brewer says that he can look out his office window every Sunday morning and see men praying in the parking lot. They pray in the vestibule and eventually gather in his office to cover him in prayer before he begins to preach. Prayer multiplies our earthly efforts and prayer magnifies our eternal endeavors.

Remember that our husbands are also the pastors of our domestic church. They need our prayers as they lead our families. Pray for their walk with God. Pray for wisdom and direction. Pray for joy as they grow to love God more and more. Praying works better than nagging. The changes that the Holy Spirit brings about in our men are for real and for keeps.

## Giving to Your Church and Pastor

Kingdom giving is one of those puzzling paradoxes of believing—a confusing contradiction in terms. Because when it comes to giving to God, the more you give, the more you get. I'm not talking about a celestial slot machine or the "Powerball" of paradise. I'm referring to the faithfulness of God to take our few loaves and fishes and feed 5,000. It's not the amount of the gift, but the attitude of the giver. "Each man should give what he has decided in his heart to give, not reluctantly or under compulsion, for God loves a cheerful giver" (2 Corinthians 9:7).

An investment of time, resources, or yourself in the work of your church or the life of your pastor is an endowment for eternity. It puts feet to your prayers. It demonstrates the honor you hold in your heart. Our service and gifts to God's work here on earth will be the standard by which God blesses us from heaven. "Give and it will be given to you. A good measure, pressed down, shaken together and running over, will be poured into your lap. For with the measure you use, it will be measured to you" (Luke 6:38).

### Give Your Time.

An enthusiastic commitment and some extra effort on your part will free your husband and family to bless someone with their time. This requires sacrifice. Your husband may not get the garbage disposal fixed this weekend if he's on a campout with his fifth-grade Sunday school class. He may not get your roses trimmed if he's across town at a single mom's home with his men's group doing her yard work and fixing her roof. This kind of sacrifice requires a cheerful giver. It's one thing to write a check; it's an entirely different matter to set aside your agenda in order to cooperate with God's.

The disintegration of the family has produced a lot of fatherless children and abandoned mothers. The church has the primary responsibility to stand in the gap and provide relief and love for these hurting souls. I always take seriously what the writer of James says: "Religion that God our Father accepts as pure and faultless is this: to look after orphans and widows in their distress and keep oneself from being polluted by the world" (James 1:27).

Encourage your husband to get involved in Awanas or the youth program at church. Men are desperately needed to mentor and model to younger children. Your family could "adopt" a needy or hurting family in your church. Invite them into your home for meals. Make sure they have their physical needs met. Whatever you can do for them frees up your pastor to help someone else.

Many churches need help keeping their facilities clean and repaired. This certainly is not a glamorous job, but it is essential. Perhaps your family could organize some other families to take this on as a ministry. It is a great way to meet others with a similar heart for service. And as a mother, I'm convinced that there has to be a crown in heaven for scrubbing and cleaning—and I'll bet it's a spotless and shiny one to reflect our efforts on earth!

### Give Your Resources.

Tim and I had about thirty minutes of pre-marital counseling. Evidently it must have been a rare time when quality won out over quantity. One of the wise gems that we took with us to the altar was the commitment to tithe. No matter how meager our income or how great our needs, we have never used God's share for our personal obligations. In telling you this, I am not looking for a pat on the back. Instead, I'm sharing with you a secret to abundant living. If you view your blessings as a means to bless others, then you are double-blessed.

Two underlying principles liberate us to give freely. The first is to remember that all that we have belongs to God; we are simply the earthly money managers. How we steward God's resources has everything to do with whether or not He entrusts us with more. And remember, *more* does not always have a dollar sign attached.

The second precept of giving is to stay out of debt. When we mortgage our future by having to spend it to finance our past, we are in bondage to debt in the present. God asks us to live below our means so we can respond when called upon to meet a need. Because of the responsibilities she carries in the home, a wife is often the biggest influence on how family money is spent. One of the best ways we can encourage our husbands to give of our resources is to keep control over the use of credit cards and stay out of debt. As we spend less, our families can afford to give more. "'Test me in this,' says the Lord Almighty, 'and see if I will not throw open the flood-gates of heaven and pour out so much blessing that you will not have room enough for it'" (Malachi 3:10).

Once your family is freed up to give, then you can experience abundant joy as God brings opportunities your way. Make sure your kids know that you cheerfully give a portion of your income to your church. They will incorporate this into their portfolio of spiritual values. Part of your Christmas giving could include a cash gift to your pastor and his family—or perhaps a gift certificate to their favorite restaurant. Don't let the IRS determine where you place your blessings. Some things are not tax deductible, but they do make a big impression in heaven. There may come a time when charitable giving loses its tax-exempt status. Will we remain faithful? I know God will.

If God has blessed your family with a cabin in the woods or a summer home at the beach, offer it to your pastor for his family vacation. Make your house or car available to the youth groups. Finance scholarships so some less fortunate kids can go to church camp. Find out what your pastor enjoys doing for recreation and then facilitate it. Let your husband take him golfing or fishing. Rick Efird told me about a family who knew that one of their church's pastors was taking his family to Disneyland. They went to the Disney Store at the mall and bought not only shirts and hats for the pastor's entire family, but also purchased their park passes. I know this pastor felt honored and appreciated.

A wife who understands why God asks us to give and how we can be freed up to give can enthusiastically support her husband as together they fulfill their commitment to be cheerful givers.

## Keeping Your Own Lantern Lit

Some of you may have already done this, but I suggest that you sit down with your husband and talk about how you can help him support your pastor and your church. How does he feel he can best do this? What can you do to help him? While you're doing this, ask God to give you understanding, humility, and a spirit of encouragement rather than criticism. Top this off with a generous portion of patience.

We must remember that none of our husbands have taken a crash course on leadership. They learn to lead in the church as they become a leader in our home. Men need to know that their leadership is appreciated no matter how small their effort. If you have a tendency to be negative, then ask God to give you a positive attitude as you dialogue with your husband. Too often, women who complain that their husbands are not assuming their role as spiritual leaders in the home have placed the same unrealistic expectations on them that people put on pastors. These husbands realize this and feel that no matter how hard they try, their wives will never be quite satisfied. Many of them, realizing the futility of it all, simply give up and do nothing.

When your husband wavers on his promises or lets you down, show him some grace by forgiving him. Ephesians 4:32 says "Be kind and compassionate to one another, forgiving each other, just as in Christ, God forgave you." We all make mistakes. When we can forgive our husbands and then offer encouragement, we stimulate them to learn from their mistakes and give them the courage to try again.

As you pray for your own spiritual growth, remember to pray for your husband's also. I have made it a habit to spend the first few minutes of my day, even before I get out of my warm bed, to pray for Tim and the challenges he faces that day. I even go so far as to spray a bit of his cologne on myself to remind me of him and his needs throughout the day. Boy, was I glad when he gave up *English Leather*.

### Nurture Your Family

My husband has one of the worst attendance records in our church. It's not that he's not in church, it's just that he's not in *our* church or even in our state many Sundays throughout the year. Weekends are when he does most of his speaking at conferences, retreats, and other churches. Even though he isn't present in our church as often as he'd like to be, we are.

I view our church as one of the stable anchors of our family life, an ally to our hearts and home. If your husband is unable to attend church, for whatever reason, make sure you go and take your children. Once again, you are modeling spiritual values. Fill your husband in on what he missed. Bring him a bulletin. Buy him a tape of the sermon. When a man knows that his commitment to his pastor and church is shared by his family, he is pleased and proud.

Choreographing a kinder and gentler Sunday morning is a challenge and a ministry for wives and mothers. I have found that if I get everything possible done the night before, including setting the table and loading the car with Bibles, it frees up vital time on Sunday morning for getting to church on time, as well as getting myself and my soul ready for worship. I am then free to assist the rest of my family as they prepare body and soul. In all aspects of supporting the mission of the church and giving time and resources to the body of Christ, a woman is often the key facilitator for her family.

### Nurture Your Christian Walk

None of the things I've talked about in this chapter are possible if a woman doesn't nourish her own spiritual life. You can't grow support, encouragement, or honor from a soul that is barren of Christ's love and teachings. If we recognize the connections between the Bible and our ability to encourage and empower our husbands, we will see that our own vital walk with God is a necessity and a spiritual service of worship (Romans 12:2).

We need to be reading and studying God's Word regularly. We need to make our life a prayer as we trust God to give us the wisdom and strength to make our greatest contributions to His Kingdom through our families. Gathering with other women who have similar goals is a great way to gain perspective and perseverance.

Tim and I were married twenty-three years ago in a beautiful church in Annapolis, Maryland. Since we have family and many friends there, we make it a point to visit them as often as we can with our children. On one of these trips several years ago, Tim had the privilege of speaking on a Sunday morning in the church we consider our home church. It's where we came to know Christ, where the foundation of our faith was laid, and where we were launched into ministry.

After the service, Tim made an appointment with our friend, Pastor Lin, to get together for breakfast two Tuesdays from then. Our family left during the middle of that week to drive to Pennsylvania for a visit with Tim's family. Tim and Lin did meet on that appointed Tuesday morning, but not for breakfast. Tim found himself at the front of this small church again. The parking lot was full, the building was packed, the sorrow was heavy. Lin and his wife, Sharon, were also there in church, side by side, as they had been for the past twenty-nine years. But this time would be their last time. They had both been killed instantly when their motorcycle hit a concrete guardrail as they came over a bridge on the freeway.

For reasons we will only know when we get to heaven, God chose to pluck them from their bike into eternity. Their sheep and fellow shepherds gathered to say good-bye. The people in that church represented their life's work: births, rebirths, baptisms, rededications, marriages, funerals, sick-bed vigils, reconciliations, souls changed by biblical teaching, their handsome son, and tender daughter-in-law. In an effort to comfort the sheep and encourage the shepherds, Tim drew the funeral to a close by asking all of the pastors from the community who'd come to honor Lin and Sharon to come forward and circle the front of the sanctuary to serve as a spiritual honor guard leading the pallbearers and caskets out of the church. These were the men and women whom Lin had loved and encouraged through his almost three decades of service to his community.

No one expected such a display of solidarity as the circle encompassed the entire front of the building. These fellow shepherds knew better than anyone else the impact of this couple's ministry and how much it would be missed. Lin and Sharon had made an eternal difference on earth and now they had gone to their eternal reward.

Life is, at best, fragile. It teeters on the fine edge of promises made and promises kept. God always keeps His promises. He will always be there to guide us when we make our promises to Him, and He will help us keep them. When all is said and done, our lives are the sum total of our devotion to God and our service to others.

Go ahead. Make that promise to your pastor and church, hand in hand with your husband, and keep it with the help of God.

### Notes

[1]"Royal Priesthood," *Leadership*, 16, no.4, (Fall 1995), p.120–123.

**Darcy Kimmel** is a child of the Great Promise
Maker, the wife of a loving Promise Keeper,
and the mother of four beautiful promises. She
speaks and writes on issues that affect the family. She dusts a lot of antique furniture, packs
a lot of lunches, and zips up a lot of suitcases.
She and her husband, Tim, live with their
four children at a bend in the road in
Scottsdale, Arizona. Darcy and Tim speak at
conferences for marriage and parenting
through Generation Ministries in Phoenix.

## Questions for Discussion

1. Describe a time when you and your husband were part of a "lantern brigade" for your pastor. How have you supported your husband in his efforts as a "lantern bearer"?

2. What is your church's mission statement? What are some specific ways your family can support this mission?

3. When was the last time you honored your pastor in a specific way? What can you do in the month ahead to honor him in one of the five ways described in this chapter?

4. Which is easier for your family to give to your church: time or resources? What can you give in the month ahead in the area in which you are weakest?

5. Sit down with your husband and discuss your thoughts on this statement: "When all is said and done, our lives are the sum total of our devotion to God and our service to others." What promises do you and your husband want to make in response to this statement?

# CHAPTER NINE

# Building Racial Bridges

KATHERYN BOONE

*R*acial prejudice is not genetic—it is taught. I know from experience. The first time I felt prejudice I was five years old. I had a deep friendship with a little girl named Kathy who was white. We were like salt and pepper. She slept over at my house and I went to hers. Both of our fathers were in the military, stationed in Germany. One day we were invited to another friend's house to see a puppet show. We were both so excited at the prospect of a fun day. We had never seen a real puppet show before.

When we arrived, the lady of the house welcomed my friend but pointed to me and said I couldn't come in. I did not understand that it was because I was black. In my little-girl mind I wondered if I was dressed inappropriately. Completely bewildered, I went home. My friend stayed.

When I got home, my mother blew up, but not in front of me. I was not aware until years later that my dad, who was two ranks higher than the father of the other family, had a meeting

with them. I'm not sure what transpired, but I know he responded to the situation. My friend left the party early and came to
my house, saying she didn't feel right there without me.

My father was a colonel at the military base, and while we
were definitely a racial minority, his rank and ability brought
respect. There are divisions that occur not only between races
and cultures, but in military ranks as well. Perhaps because of
my father's rank and station, I may not have experienced as
much prejudice as other blacks in the service. But I can still
remember the bewilderment and hurt I felt about why I
couldn't do some of the things my white friends could.

## Viewing Race Through God's Eyes

Those things happened years ago. Our country is no longer
*legally* segregated, and prejudice is no longer as widespread as it
was when I was growing up. Much is happening in the culture
at large. I'm amazed at how many books have been written on
reconciliation.

But despite all the rhetoric, we have miles to go in bringing
about true racial reconciliation. We keep growing apart. As
recently as November, 1995, President Clinton said he was
considering appointing a panel to study the nation's racial
divide.

Division surrounds us, even in God's family. There have
been longstanding traditional barriers, spoken and unspoken,
overt and implied, between races within churches. It is said
that eleven o'clock on Sunday morning is the most segregated
hour of the week. During that hour in many churches, like-
minded people gather and refuse emotional or relational entry
to any who are different and may threaten the status quo.

We witness churches splitting, families splitting, and

nations splitting over issues of race. However, this was never God's intent. As Christians we are to follow after the character, not color, of Jesus. Heaven will be multicolored, for God's children are from every race. If Adam had been faithful to the dominion God entrusted to him in the Garden, there would be no prejudice, no racial and cultural tensions today. Sin has lingering consequences. Yet through the second Adam, Jesus Christ, perfect love went to the cross and gave us the opportunity to be reconciled to God and to each other.

Perhaps you're reading this and thinking, *I don't have a problem with prejudice. What's the big deal?* In response I'd like to tell you about a *Star Trek* episode which I think suggests how God views prejudice.

The *Starship Enterprise* had picked up two men from a distant planet. One had been pursuing the other for many years. He told Captain Kirk that the man he was pursuing was wanted for crimes he had committed in their world. On this particular planet, some of the citizens' faces were white on the right side and black on the left, while the tone of the others was a mirror image: black on the right and white on the left. This subtle difference had led part of the population to assume a position of superiority, and the factions had been at war for centuries.

The man doing the pursuing considered himself from the master race. At one point in the episode he was trying unsuccessfully to convince the crew that he was superior to his countryman. He asked Spock, "Are you blind? Can you not see?"

Spock replied, "No, you're black on one side and white on the other side."

"But I'm black on the left side and white on the right, and he's the opposite," the man responded in frustration.

Captain Kirk and his crew were unable to distinguish the difference. To them the people of the planet were all white on one side, black on the other. What difference did it make which side was which? In Kirk's mind the important thing was that they were all the same beneath the color of their skin.

At the end of the show, the two men beamed down to their planet, only to find it completely destroyed. The hate and prejudice of their society had ended in destruction.

There is a lesson here for us. While prejudice between Christians is very subtle, we too have made assessments on the basis of each other's skin color. I suspect that God views our division much like Captain Kirk and his crew saw these two men. God should not have to make us look alike in order for us to get along. He made us different to complement each other, just as He made red and white and pink carnations which mix magnificently. We need to see all people as God sees all that He created: good! Otherwise, we do great damage to each other and thwart God's purposes.

There is no place for racial barriers in the family of God. The Word tells us that He has called His children to be one with Him and with each other. In order for His will to be realized, we must first unite. To unite simply means to join. We must become unified in our efforts toward reconciliation.

## Encouraging Your Husband in Racial Reconciliation

I want to be the woman God wants me to be and assist Wellington in obeying God's will. However, I would be less than honest if I said it was easy and comes naturally. Like most women, I have the tendency to want to remake and remold. It's critical for me to spend time in the Word and in prayer so the Lord can show me when I need to get out of the way and permit Him to do what is right.

As a wife I am first responsible to the Lord and then to the man I married. That is really something to try to live up to—an impossible task without the help of my Father. He often reminds me that whom He calls, He enables. God alone enables me to help and encourage a highly motivated, dedicated, and determined husband to keep his promises to the only father he has truly known: God.

Wellington is called to keep his promises to God, and I to seek God on his behalf and be that help God ordained me to be. Together we seek to bring racial reconciliation. We are both convinced that blacks can reach whites and whites can reach blacks. How? Through knowing what was in the heart of God when He created man and then modeling the words of Jeremiah 29:11: "'For I know the plans I have for you,' declares the Lord, 'plans to prosper you and not to harm you, plans to give you hope and a future.'"

Those words were not addressed just to whites or just to blacks or Asians or Hispanics; they are a statement of God's unconditional love for the whole world He created. There is no need for affirmative action with God. Our position was already settled at the cross. But because of the cross, we are called to take that reconciliation to our neighbors, our cities, and the world.

Wellington often says that blacks are blessed beyond measure because they have had training to serve others. With this intuitive knowledge, they have the ability to minister to all cultures, not from a position of servitude, but in submission to God's will and purpose. God's message to the Pharaoh of Egypt is needed today as we challenge the pharaoh of racism:

*Let My people go!* Once steps toward reconciliation have been initiated within the ranks of our churches and denominations, we can move on to a parallel course with God in reaching out to the rest of the world.

You may be thinking that this issue is too big, that you can't influence it. While it may be true that only God can bring about the deep healing that is needed, it's not true that you and your family are powerless. Healing reconciliation begins with a prayerful awareness and concern about the divisive issue of race relations and a desire to align our hearts with God's heart.

## Changing Attitudes and Ideas That Create Barriers

Barriers are obstructions that separate or hinder. Reconciliation begins when barriers are torn down. The feeling that one race is superior to another is a barrier that has to be broken down before reconciliation can begin.

It's important that we realize that barriers do not arise accidentally or overnight. Building barriers takes skill and practice. They're made from subtle attitudes, ideas and concepts, even lifestyles, that reflect the barrier in every way. Sometimes we find ourselves behind barriers of other people's making.

Regardless of the source or cause, we need to recognize racist attitudes and ideas for what they are. We need to scrutinize each one, asking, *Does this reflect Jesus' character?* If not, we need to be willing to begin the process of dismantling it. Again, dismantling barriers takes skill and must be intentional. The intent is to make sure that our attitudes, ideas, concepts, and lifestyles reflect Jesus' character in every way.

But where do we start? With Jesus, of course.

*Ask yourself how Jesus sees race.*

Galatians 3:28–29 says, "There is neither Jew nor Greek, slave nor free, male nor female, for you are all one in Christ Jesus. And if you belong to Christ, then you are Abraham's seed, and heirs according to the promise." In other words, we are all His children, and He does not see race as a point of division, but only as a reflection of His creativity.

Think about your own family. Would you treat your red-headed daughter different from your blonde? Would you make one daughter live in the barn and the other in the house, just because of their hair color? Of course not. If I asked you why, you would probably tell me, "It makes no difference. They're both my children, and besides, they had nothing to do with the color of their hair. God made that decision."

Once you and I begin to see humankind, and our Christian brothers and sisters in particular, the same way we see our own families, we'll have taken the first step in seeing from God's perspective. Christians, no matter their skin color, are *all* in God's family.

*Recognize that we need to offer each other forgiveness.*

It is time for blacks and whites to reconcile with each other, to stop making racism a scapegoat and whipping boy for all that is wrong between us. We need to stop saying that we just can't get together because our cultures are different. It's time to abandon our stereotypes and generalizations and to let go of past grievances. It's time to "make friendly again, to settle or compose or to bring into harmony."[1] It's time to reconcile.

Without mutual forgiveness, without seeing the plank in our own eye as well as the speck in our brother's, true reconciliation is impossible. Acquittal is one-sided forgiveness and exculpation.

It is necessary to acquit those who have been guilty of wrongdoing toward us before we can reach a state of vindication or mutual forgiveness. When forgiveness is mutual, both parties extend it because both share guilt. In offering mutual forgiveness, we tear down a barrier and move toward reconciliation.

We should strive to have a patience like God's. We should be long-suffering, reluctant to punish, capable of forgetting an injury and ignoring a wrong, whether recent or in the past. This, simply put, is the character of God. We should be willing to be a bridge between those of all races, leading to God the Father. While white and black Christians may have differences, our common spiritual ground is our belief in God and that reconciliation is a ministry given to the church (2 Corinthians 5:18).

### Recognize that we are one in the body of Christ.

Years ago when I asked Wellington to attend church with me, we heard Jack R. Taylor, a staunch, strict Baptist preacher visiting in town. Spellbound during the service, Wellington was touched by God. It was the beginning of an intense commitment that's hard to define. He had finally reached the place described by the hymn: "I have decided to follow Jesus. No turning back. No turning back."

Throughout our married life, we've discovered that the ground is level at the foot of the cross. In Jesus, gender, denomination, race, and culture are not important. He is Father of all. We are complete in Him. We are one in the body of Christ.

I have black and white friends who "love me to shreds." They love me, not because of my color, but because of my heart and spirit. We need to teach our children that while human beings look at our outward appearance, God looks at our hearts (1 Samuel 16:7). Our color is God's prerogative. We need to be one in the bond of His love. Heaven will have no foolishness. We will not be black or Caucasian or Hispanic or Asian; we will simply be God's children in the Kingdom that is being prepared for us, where we will reign with Him forever.

**Focus on what we have in common.**

Let's find points to agree on and let go of the petty stuff that keeps us apart. We need to realize anew we are chosen of God, heirs of God, and joint heirs with Christ. A royal priesthood. A chosen generation. We are not better than one another, just different. When God enables us to change our hearts and our attitudes, we are better able to take some practical steps that will promote reconciliation between races.

## Hospitality Builds a Bridge

More and more blacks are moving away from the goal of integration and assimilation into a multi-racial community and are putting distance between themselves and the cultural, social, economic, and political norms of white America. They are not willing to immerse themselves in a hostile world just for the sake of being integrated.

This call by blacks for isolation is nothing new. As far back as the 1780s, there were blacks who urged black citizens to leave the United States to move back to Africa or the Caribbean to escape white institutions. But when this attitude prevails, the hope of a colorblind society fades.

How can this trend be reversed? One small way is through hospitality and opening our homes and lives to others. The Bible gives us many illustrations of hospitable people. In

Genesis 18 an unaware Abraham entertained angels. Who knows what effect our befriending someone of another race or culture may have on their future accomplishments or the direction of their lives? Abigail touched David's heart by being hospitable. The widow at Zarephath showed kindness to Elijah, and David cared for Meshibosheth by bringing him to his table.

The New Testament chronicles the stories of Mary and Martha and others who cared for the saints. In 1 Timothy 3:2 the requirements for leaders and bishops (my husband) are the characteristics of being "temperate, self-controlled, respectable, hospitable, able to teach…." Because my husband has the biblical assignment of hospitality, we work together as a team to minister hospitality in our home, church, and other places.

In 1 Peter 4:8–10 we are challenged: "Above all, love each other deeply, because love covers a multitude of sins. Offer hospitality to one another without grumbling. Each one should use whatever gift he has received to serve others, faithfully administering God's grace in its various forms."

I believe that one of the most effective ways a wife can help her husband in promoting reconciliation is by opening their home to people from other races, both friends and strangers. Understanding can come through fellowship and hospitality. A cup of cold water does not go unrewarded, nor does a batch of cookies. Small acts of practical kindness can be the window through which God's unconditional love can shine.

Inviting people into your home is like opening your heart to God's plan. There is something about a living room that puts people at ease and says "you are important." Sitting together at a table can be both relaxing and revealing. A camaraderie develops.

An attorney and his wife invited Wellington and me over to their lovely home—the antithesis of ours at the time. Although our skin was a different color, we were warmly welcomed. They worked with us, encouraged us, and admonished us to do likewise.

I am convinced that by being hospitable I can help Wellington keep his promises to God to help bring about racial reconciliation. After all, just as Jesus is the Host of heaven, we are to host His family on earth. I believe that such occasions strengthen bonds and love between people. Never wait until everything is just right. It never will be. Start today. You never know what God might do.

A heartening story illustrates this truth. A friend of mine was teaching a Bible study for an ill pastor. She asked those attending to put their suggestions for the summer series in a box. One person requested that they study the twenty-third Psalm. On one Wednesday the teacher was discussing the phrase, "You prepare a table before me in the presence of my enemies" (v. 5). She told about some times when she had been unkind, overbearing, or brittle to others. She had apologized to the people she had hurt by inviting them out for coffee, lunch, or even to her home for dinner.

The following Wednesday night, one of the black women spoke up when the Bible study began and asked to share an incident that had happened to her that week. She related how her angry white neighbor had approached her, delivering a tirade about her daughter destroying some flowers in the flowerbed next door while retrieving a ball. The white neighbor, full of vitriol, punctuated her tirade with expletives, saying she wished the black family had never moved in. They had ruined everything!

The black woman remembered the verse from the previous Bible study about preparing a table in the presence of an enemy. Once the neighbor stopped yelling, she invited her over for coffee so they could discuss the child's destructive actions. Much to her surprise, the woman accepted and said she'd be over in a few minutes.

The black woman quickly put some flowers on the living room coffee table, rinsed out two of her best china cups and saucers, and set the kettle on to boil. She put some home-made cookies on a plate and placed it on the table just as the doorbell rang. The setting for hospitality surprised the neighbor and she reluctantly sat down.

The hostess suggested they pray for God's wisdom in how to handle the incident. While the neighbor did not want a prayer, she didn't resist. At the end, she was sobbing. She explained how her life was in shambles, full of family struggles and financial woes. The Christian hostess shared the Lord and extended an invitation to Bible study. The neighbor accepted. The subject of the thoughtless daughter was never even brought up.

While the two women were talking, a man who was hanging draperies in the dining room overheard their conversation. When the neighbor left, he asked if God could help with his problems, too. He was a Korean, married to a white woman, and they were struggling to find acceptance in the community.

Two weeks later both the neighbor and the drapery hanger and his wife were in church. By the end of the summer, all had accepted Jesus as Savior. Soon an interracial explosion of God's love permeated the group. Why? Because someone was willing to set a table in the name of the Lord.

## A Spiritual Issue

I have learned that racial harmony will not trickle down, it must rise up from within us. Racism is not a governmental or political problem; it is a spiritual one. And Christians have the answer.

As Wellington's wife, I am committed to reaching beyond any racial, cultural, denominational, or gender barrier. I want to be a living demonstration of the power of the unity of the Spirit and the bond of peace. I want to uphold Wellington and his vision that we all enlarge our circle of love in the body of Christ, making sure no one is excluded. It is a big order, but we serve a big God.

I pray to God that when I face Him before His eternal throne, He will find me faithful in living up to my potential and the promises I made to Him. We have come so far in bringing about racial reconciliation, but there is still so much to be done.

Racial reconciliation is a possible dream. It can be achieved, but it's up to us as members of God's forever family to meet the issues head-on and be players in the process. As the body of Christ we are to become the breeding ground of compassionate hearts, alive with the word of reconciliation and at work in the ministry of reconciliation.

Reconciliation is not a destination, it is a journey. Will you join in the high calling of changing hearts, one at a time?

### Notes

[1] *Webster's New Universal Unabridged Dictionary*, © 1983,1955

**Katheryn Boone** is the wife of Wellington Boone and the mother of Jason, Nicole, and Justin. She has assisted her husband in establishing several churches as well as many outreach ministries, including Wellington Boone Ministries, Network of Christian Women, New Generation Campus/Youth United Ministries, and Network of Politically Active Christian Women.

## Questions for Discussion

1. What are some of the subtle ways racial prejudice shows up in your life? What have you read in this chapter that most inspires you to examine your heart and behavior?

2. What are some ways you and your husband can intentionally tear down barriers between yourselves and people of different races? Can you give an example of a time you did this successfully?

3. Have you ever had an experience with someone of a different race that increased your prejudice? If so, describe the incident and how you felt about it. What can you do now to overcome the barriers this experience has erected in your heart?

4. Do you have regular opportunities to interact with people of different races or cultures? If not, what can you do to be part of the ministry of reconciliation described in this chapter?

5. Describe a time when you extended hospitality to someone of a different race or culture. What did you learn? If you haven't extended hospitality to people in other ethnic groups, will you commit to doing so in the month ahead?

# CHAPTER TEN

# *Influencing Our World for Christ*

PATRICIA M. PALAU

*W*hat does it take to be a woman of influence?

Have you ever dreamed of God, using you to make a difference in people's lives? Or caught a vision for how God might use you and your husband to "go and make disciples of all nations" (Matthew 28:19)?

After graduating from Seattle Pacific University, I taught in a public school and dreamed of getting married and serving God overseas. The next year, I recommitted myself to the Lord's service, even if that meant staying single the rest of my life, and pursued graduate theological studies at what is now Multnomah Biblical Seminary.

Luis Palau was headstrong, confident, and single-minded when we met at Multnomah during the fall of 1960. He knew exactly what lay ahead after his graduate studies: he planned to return to South America as a missionary with Overseas Crusades. I too had made a decision: I'd given up looking for Mr. Right and looked forward to teaching missionary children in Taiwan. But by spring semester Luis and I had fallen in love.

As we were walking together under an umbrella in the rain, Luis popped the big question. No, not, "Will you marry me?" but, "Will you go with me to South America?"

I knew what that entailed, and he knew what my "yes" meant. I chose to submit my will to God's call on Luis to preach the gospel to people around the world. From the beginning, evangelism was the focal point of our marriage.

## Benefits of an Outward Focus

At that time I wasn't aware of all that an international ministry of itinerant evangelism would involve (extensive travel, lengthy separations, and mothering four boys alone at least a third of the time), but I *did* know that Luis was a man of no small vision. God wants everyone to be saved (1 Timothy 2:4), and there have been times when I thought my husband was determined to do his best to reach the last four billion lost souls for Jesus Christ.

Our lifestyle isn't for everybody; my husband is an evangelist to whom God has given opportunities beyond our wildest dreams. But I believe our marriage has been strengthened as we've reached out to others with the gospel. Working together to bring the Good News to all people has helped us keep our focus outward instead of inward.

We've never entertained such questions as, *Should Luis move into a more financially rewarding career?* or, *When will we be able to afford a nicer home?* For the first few years of our marriage, we lived in three different countries. Owning our own home wasn't even an option. We expected things to be different from the norm. We also knew up front that we couldn't meet each other's needs 100 percent. That realization protected us from disappointments that result from unrealistic expectations.

But looking back, I feel somehow we've achieved many of the goals other couples struggle toward for years, such as working together well to successfully raise four sons. I may be reading a magazine article about typical marriage conflicts and suddenly I find myself thinking, *What do you know? Even though Luis has had to travel so much over the years, somehow we've avoided those specific, common marital pitfalls.*

Perhaps some things are improved by a lack of inward focus. Instead of focusing on our marriage or our desires, Luis and I have focused on the call of God on our lives. We have lived for a cause that's bigger than both of us. And after thirty-five years, we like each other, get along well, and have fulfilled one another as much as is possible.

Our fulfillment is doing the will of God. Our heart prayer is, *Not my will, Lord, but Yours.* This focus kept me from saying, "I deserve more help than this" when Luis has been gone for two weeks, leaving me with four little boys. I didn't think, *I can't believe Luis has to leave again so soon,* two or three weeks after his last trip. For me, the Lord's command to "take up your cross and follow Me" has meant letting Luis go while I take care of things at home. No, it isn't "fair," but it brings life—eternal life—to others. And I gain peace, contentment, and satisfaction.

## Not Just for Pros

As you read this chapter, you may be tempted to think, *I'm going to work on my Bible study and prayer because they're basic to my faith. But witnessing—evangelism—that's for the pros. It's not for me until I'm more spiritually mature.* It's true that some discipleship programs seem to follow this principle: we can't reach out with the gospel because we're not mature enough. But I'm convinced that when we tell others what we know, when we're willing to be the beggar telling the other beggar where to find bread, we're doing ourselves far more good than we realize. The strongest believers I know began immediately to share what they knew as brand new Christians, and other parts of their Christian walk have fallen in line. As we share the gospel with others, we become more spiritually mature. It's not *either/or*; it's *both/and*.

We will stimulate and develop other areas of our Christian life as we strive to obey God in this area. We don't have to take evangelism classes to learn how to witness for Christ, although it's good to learn to articulate the basics of our faith. So what if we mess up the first time or two? God is still in control. No one will ever go to hell because we did something wrong. It is essential that we get to work immediately on telling others what we know.

Interestingly, although they are often the most clumsy witnesses, new believers are usually the best at it. Why? Because they know how to talk to non-Christians. They need no reminder of what it was like to be lost, and therefore they feel a tremendous sense of urgency to share the Good News of salvation.

## What's **Really** Important?

As one of Luis's evangelistic campaigns in Scotland came to an end in 1980, I discovered a suspicious warning sign of cancer. We immediately flew home and I saw a specialist that Friday. Our worst fears were confirmed: I had cancer. We spent the weekend trying to absorb the shock. The following Monday I had radical surgery and then began two years of chemotherapy. It was dreadful. I remember thinking, *How does a person outside of Christ deal with a potentially terminal illness?* Evangelism grew much more urgent in my mind.

At the suggestion of the medical personnel at the hospital, I attended a coping-with-cancer support group for a few weeks. It was a hopeless affair. Someone in the group would talk about "coming to terms with the fact that I'm terminal" without any reference to God or hope beyond this life. But I shouldn't have been surprised. Secular authorities on facing death advise people to "come to terms with death" or to adopt an approach that says, "Things might get better, after all; everything always does. If not, what can I do about it, anyway? I just need to roll with the punches."

In the midst of battling cancer, I came to more fully understand that people need to know about the Lord because we're all terminal. More than ever, I understood that the only thing that's really worth living for is telling people about Jesus Christ. It doesn't mean it's the only thing you do twenty-four hours a day, but it's what's behind what you do. "Why do you put up with your husband leaving you behind while he preaches?" you ask. Because it's for a greater good. It's part of embracing Jesus' clear statement: "For whoever wants to save his life will lose it, but whoever loses his life for me and for the gospel will save it" (Mark 8:35).

Discovering I had cancer was a tremendous shock. I realized it was one thing to know something mentally and another to know it experientially. Having cancer helped me see areas of unbelief in my life. One false belief was an indomitable self-reliance: *I am very smart. I am very gifted. I can do anything.* Cancer takes that right out of you. It points a finger toward eternity, bringing home the truth that no matter how you cut it, we're not getting out of here alive. It's only a matter of time. If I escape the ravages of cancer, someday something else is going to get me. One poem puts it this way:

> Only one life will soon be past.
> Only what's done for Christ will last.

## Never, Never, Never Give Up

Over the years, Luis has proclaimed the gospel to some twelve million people in sixty-three nations. Now that all our boys are grown and married, I travel with him. But nothing I do in support of my husband's ministry replaces my own responsibility to witness, although I'm sure evangelism is not my spiritual gift. Being a witness is a personal responsibility, not something we can delegate to others, not even to our husbands.

My years as an evangelist's wife have taught me the need to persevere in my commitment to influence the world for the Lord. Those of us who have been Christians a long time can easily let this commitment wane. We need biblical reminders in order to persevere.

We are an impatient generation. We want circumstances to change *now*. We want evidence that God is working in our lives and in the lives of the people closest to us. We don't have time to wait in prayer. We want results—instantly.

In contrast, in the Bible we read such words as *perseverance* and *patience*. We are encouraged to "throw off everything that hinders and the sin that so easily entangles, and...run with perseverance the race marked out for us" (Hebrews 12:1). If we insist on "feeling good" all the time, we'll never understand the heartbeat of the mission of Jesus, who "did not come to be served, but to serve, and to give his life as a ransom for many" (Mark 10:45). God calls us to compassion for the lost. In the end, nothing makes us "feel" as good as does obedience to Him.

We must stick with what God tells us to do until He tells us to stop. I guarantee He will never tell us to stop loving the people in the world and taking the gospel to them because He never stops loving and pursuing those whom He created in His image. "But do not forget this one thing, dear friends: With the Lord a day is like a thousand years, and a thousand years are like a day. The Lord is not slow in keeping his promise, as some understand slowness. He is patient with you, not wanting anyone to perish, but everyone to come to repentance" (2 Peter 3:8–9).

God never gives up. To Him, no amount of time is too long to pray for someone—nor should it be to us. "Let us not become weary in doing good, for at the proper time we will reap a harvest if we do not give up" (Galatians 6:9). The Bible says we shall reap at the proper time, but it doesn't say how long we'll have to wait for our proper time to arrive. What if we must wait a lifetime? So be it. We have God's absolute promise that He will work out His will in our lives.

Luis and I know an elderly woman who prayed for sixty-eight years for her brother's salvation. He received Christ when he was eighty years old, shortly before he died. You may think, *That was by the skin of his teeth!* But not to God. Imagine the tremendous blessings resulting from sixty-eight years of praying.

For years Luis and I have prayed for the salvation of certain unsaved relatives. One nephew trusted Christ a few months before dying of AIDS. Other, older family members still haven't committed their lives to Him. They're getting quite elderly now, and we're concerned. It's quite possible some may keep putting off a decision until the last minute. That's in God's hands. But no matter how long it takes, we'll keep praying.

### Partners in Evangelism

Whenever possible, we should evangelize with our husbands, whether it's by witnessing to our next-door neighbor or the governor of our state. Luis and I know a Dutch couple who lived near The Hague and attended many peace conferences during the Cold War. The Van Eegans had a beautiful farm in the country where they raised horses. During the peace conferences they would befriend Russian military leaders, and then ask, "Would you like to come out and spend a Saturday with us?" The men would ride horses together, and then come back to the house to converse and enjoy a nice meal.

One day a four-star Russian general and a KGB agent accepted this couple's invitation to visit their farm. Partway through the day, Mr. and Mrs. Van Eegan split up the two men. It was obvious the KGB agent was "protecting" the Russian general from any "undue" influences. So Mr. Van Eegan took him aside and talked in one room while Mrs. Van Eegan talked with the general.

As soon as she was alone with the Russian general, Mrs. Van Eegan told him, "You must be a child of God."

"What are you talking about?"

"You're here for the peace conference, right? The Bible says, 'Blessed are the peacemakers, for they shall be called the children of God.'" She was using this Bible verse out of context, of course, but to make an important point.

To her shock, the general started to weep. Mrs. Van Eegan asked what was the matter. "My mother used to quote that verse to me when I was a boy," he told her.

"So, do you know God?"

"No, I don't, but I have always wanted to know Him, especially since my mother died."

"Sir, you can know God right here, today." Mrs. Van Eegan explained the gospel to this general and led him to the Lord a few minutes later while her husband kept the KGB agent preoccupied in the other room.

Several months later, Mr. Van Eegan had an opportunity to visit the general while in Moscow on business. Not only was the general growing in the things of the Lord, he was leading a Bible study with eight or ten other Russian military officers!

God can use you and your husband, together, to reach people at all levels of society for Jesus Christ. Sometimes your husband will be in the driver's seat; sometimes you'll need to take a more active role. When it's your turn, don't hesitate to love someone to the Savior.

Luis and I know a young couple, Tom and Lisa, who serve as missionaries in Singapore. Lisa has an Italian background and Tom is a quiet northern European. They work great together. They support one another, but Lisa is the more outgoing of the two. Not long ago she had an opportunity to go to Colombia to speak at a conference. Tom immediately encouraged her, "You go ahead. I'll take care of the children. This is a great opportunity." I thought that was terrific. It got Lisa out where God could use her in some new and powerful ways.

## Three Stages of Opportunity

Most married couples work through three stages in their obedience to Christ's command to make disciples of all nations: before they have children, while they have children, and after their children have grown up. Each stage has opportunities.

### Stage 1: Before Children

Our sons are all married. Two, Andrew and Stephen, are not yet fathers. I've noticed that Andrew and his wife, Wendy, who live near us in Portland, Oregon, are aggressive in outreach together. Because they have fewer distractions than does a couple with children, they can put a lot of time into friendships with non-Christians. They invest considerable time in maintaining friendships and doing things with their friends. Because they spend time really getting to know non-Christians, they are comfortable inviting them to attend an evangelistic outreach at church or in the community.

### Stage 2: With Children

My greatest evangelistic opportunity came during the stage when my boys were at home. Parents must set as their greatest goal evangelizing their own children. Do children somehow become Christians by osmosis? Hardly! God has no grandchildren. Yet we've met sincere people who say, "I was born into a Christian family," or "I've been a Christian all my life." As parents, we need to dispel our children's misconceptions about what it means to be a Christian and demonstrate that we deeply care whether or not they make a genuine commitment to Jesus Christ. We can't make that decision for anybody, but as Christian parents we can have an active part in leading our sons and daughters to faith in Christ.

Proverbs 11:30 says, "The fruit of the righteous is a tree of life, and he [or she] who wins souls is wise." Parents always try to teach their children important lessons in life, to provide a good education, and build self-esteem. Don't forget to give your children to Jesus, first and foremost. They are never too young to come to Him. The Lord longs to welcome children into His family. "Let the little children come to me," Jesus said, "and do not hinder them, for the kingdom of heaven belongs to such as these" (Matthew 19:14). No, they don't understand all the concepts, but we are bringing them to Him and they are accepting all they know. That's all Luis and I have ever done, and that's been plenty good enough. The greatest joy you can know is to see your children trust the Lord Jesus as Savior.

Your children will open doors to reach other children and their parents for Christ. When Andrew was little, two mothers showed up on my doorstep one morning. Their children were Andrew's best friends. Neither had been near a church in years, and they had a lot of questions. I was able to lead them to the Lord. I would not have had that opportunity were it not for Andrew's friendliness.

When our sons were growing up, Luis and I always chose "the children in evangelism, not the children versus evangelism." Ministry was a family affair. I realized my attitude made all the difference for my children. I wanted to communicate to them, *This isn't just something your daddy's doing—we're doing it as a family. Isn't this exciting? We all win people to Jesus. We're all in this together.*

### Stage 3: After Children

When our children are grown, another stage of life presents itself in which there are many active things we can do if we choose to get into the thick of things. For me, that involves traveling with Luis'much more than was possible before our youngest son, Stephen, went away to college. Even then I waited for several months. I wanted the first Christmas Stephen came back home to feel as normal as possible. I didn't want him thinking, *Wow, my mom couldn't wait for me to get out of the house*.

Some have asked me, "Isn't it great to travel so much and speak to so many people?" Glamorous it is not. It gets old fast! It's still a sacrifice every time Luis and I have to leave home, even though the children are grown up. If it weren't for the sake of the gospel, we'd much rather stay home, thank you. But long ago we discovered there's nothing more exciting, more thrilling, or more rewarding than to help spread the gospel to all people. People without Christ are truly lost. They are headed for a Christless eternity. It is urgent that we offer them Jesus' Good News.

Each of us has a role. Encourage your husband to do his part. Don't hold him back. And do all you can to make an eternal difference in people's lives.

## Offering Wholehearted Support

When I said yes to Luis and chose to submit my will to God's call on his life, I began a supportive role. Being supportive is biblical. It may mean taking a secondary role in other people's eyes, but remember, *your choice to support your husband's call means a greater good can be accomplished*.

I support my husband in his direct exercise of his spiritual gift: evangelism. Supporting your spouse's spiritual gift is a positive, worthwhile goal. "Submit to one another out of reverence for Christ" (Ephesians 5:21).

I cannot deny that supporting Luis has meant sacrificing. Separations bring loss. Separations take adjustments. There is no point in saying you will make up for them. I used to say that and defend that point of view, but in the end I had to admit, "Well, yes, there is a loss." You can't have everything. There are probably ways in which, as a couple, Luis and I don't know each other fully. There are things we didn't get to do. Some interests must be set aside, and I've found myself thinking, *I'll never know if I would have been good at that.* But I made a choice, and my choice meant there would be things I could not pursue. When I catch myself thinking, *I probably could do this better if I put more attention into it,* I remember that I deliberately choose not to pay more attention in that area. There's a limit to what I can do. I have only so much energy.

## A Personal Commitment

I often ask myself, *What will it take for Luis to exercise his spiritual gift for a lifetime? What does it demand from me?*

Twenty years ago I wrote a personal statement that I review from time to time and recommit myself to. It's not for everybody; it's mine. This is what it says:

> I want to be known as a totally traditional supportive wife and mother, who loves God and His Word, who values truth above all else, with four sons who will bless their generation and a husband to whose ministry I contribute

169

not just the benefits of an orderly home, but
the result of consistent and progressive study
of God's Word. My satisfaction and self-worth
shall come from hearing the results of my
research and my input in his evangelistic sermons. I'd like to be thought of as a woman
who thinks, can be trusted with ideas—not to
push the limits or to prove something, but for
my own sake and for the benefit of those
whose lives I touch, directly or indirectly.

Today I resist the urge to edit that statement. At the time,
it expressed something deep in my heart. I probably wrote it
at a time when women were beginning to emphasize, *Don't let
him do it to you...don't knuckle under to anybody.... What? You
have all that education and this is what you do? Why don't you
pursue your own ministry?*

I remember reading one article that said, in effect: "It's
okay for the average Christian woman to support her spouse,
but the multi-gifted woman will find such an arrangement far
too frustrating and completely unworkable." That was insult-
ing. It offended me. I've thought it through, and what I do
with Luis really is the best use of my life. In the end, I will
accomplish more by supporting God's call on Luis than by trying to go out and do my own thing. This is God's "thing" for
me. That's what my personal statement is all about.

I also believe my statement reflects the very character and
person of Jesus Christ developing in me (Galatians 2:20). I
am committed to persevere to the end. I will never quit or
retire from representing Jesus Christ. I don't say, "I did that
for a while. Now I'm moving on to something else."

Evangelism is for a lifetime. It's a lifestyle, not a little project we take a shot at and abandon when it's not fun.

## What About You?

Do you want to be a woman of influence? Together with your husband, do you want to draw others to the Savior?

I urge you to make a wholehearted commitment to obeying Christ's commands to love others and take the gospel to all nations through every stage of your marriage, come what may. Record your commitment in a written personal statement and review it often.

Keep this promise and watch the Lord revolutionize your world for His glory.

**Pat Palau** has enjoyed a growing sphere of ministry in recent years, both as a public speaker and as an author of articles published in *Christian Parenting Today, Focus on the Family, Moody,* and many other periodicals. She's also the co-author of *How to Lead Your Child to Christ* (Multnomah Press) and a contributing author of *How to Keep Your Kids Christian* (Vine Books).

## Questions for Discussion

1. How much of a focus is evangelism in your marriage? In what ways do you each feel "called" to minister to others, and how are you living out these callings?

2. Do either you or your husband consider evangelism to be one of your spiritual gifts? Do you consider evangelism to be your personal responsibility as a Christian? Why or why not? What impact does your belief have on your choices in life?

3. Have you and your husband witnessed as a team? If so, what did you do, and what were the results?

4. Which "stage" is your marriage in with regard to Christ's command to make disciples of all nations? Do you think you are experiencing your greatest opportunity to evangelize now, or is that stage to come? How can you prepare for it?

5. In what ways have you sacrificed some of your personal goals and wishes in order to support God's call on your husband? How do you feel about this? Do you see how your choices to support your husband's call have resulted in a greater good being accomplished?

# CHAPTER ELEVEN

# When He Doesn't Keep His Promises

MARTIE STOWELL

*H*e promised he'd be home for a special dinner with the whole family and you worked hard to get the house clean and cook his favorite meal. Right before 5:00 he calls to say he has an emergency and won't be home until late. Disappointed and angry, you make excuses to the children and try to make the dinner enjoyable for them despite your feelings. You put the kids to bed and try to read a book, all the while thinking of what you're going to say when he finally walks in the door.

It's happened to every wife. We've all experienced the pain of a broken promise.

My husband is a godly man who loves me and makes me feel secure. I don't believe Joe would ever intentionally hurt me. But he has an incredibly difficult schedule, and sometimes an unexpected problem arises that requires his immediate attention. When this happens it can cause all sorts of havoc with our plans and my expectations.

As much as we might wish it were otherwise, the fact is we live in a fallen world. Joe and I are both sinners saved by the miracle of Christ's love, and despite our best intentions we sometimes fail each other. This doesn't take away the pain of a broken promise, but it does allow me to keep in mind that God is working in both our lives to make us more like Christ.

Some of you have struggled with disappointments similar to mine. Your husband works too much or perhaps he fails to let you know about plans he's made that impact you. Others of you have experienced far greater disappointment than I. Perhaps your husband has broken his marriage vows and has had an affair. Or perhaps he has abused you repeatedly, always promising never to do so again. My heart goes out to you and I hope to offer you some guidelines that will help you gain perspective and hope. I have seen God do amazing things even in marriages that seemed doomed.

I believe there is a series of questions a woman can ask herself that will apply to every one of these difficult situations. Whether you are weathering a major catastrophe or working out the little details of married life, you'll find these questions helpful as you focus on keeping God's perspective in the midst of a broken promise.

## Did He Really Break His Promise to Me?

When Joe and I became engaged, I had a set of assumptions about how our married life would be. One of those was that Joe would be home most evenings and we'd spend hours together talking, sharing activities, and dreaming together, just like we did when we were dating. But those expectations didn't materialize. After we were married, Joe juggled seminary, a part-time job, and a ministry assignment in addition to his commitment to me as his wife. He often came home late and I would be upset about having to spend the evening without him after working hard all day at my frustrating job. I felt Joe was breaking some unspoken promise about spending time with me. But you see, that was the problem: I never spoke with him about my expectations. In my mind he was breaking a promise, but in his mind he was simply fulfilling his responsibilities.

Christian management author Bobb Biehl says that "all miscommunications are the result of differing assumptions." The longer I think about that statement, the more I agree with it. A wife has assumptions about time with her husband, about money, about meals, and about the children. Her husband has different assumptions. So every time he acts in some way that differs from her assumptions, she feels as though he's broken a promise to her. But that really isn't the case. When this happens a couple needs to talk through their assumptions and expectations so that they can come to agreement on the important issues in their marriage.

One couple I know has always haggled about money. The husband was raised in a family that saved money for things and then bought them, but the wife's family saved money just to save money. They rarely bought anything. So when her husband comes walking in the door with some small item he's purchased, she gets angry about his "high-living ways."

But through talking about their expectations and backgrounds, they were finally able to come to an agreement. They decided that if they wanted to buy something that cost more than fifteen dollars, they would discuss it and come to an agreement. The husband was happy, since he felt his wife was now on his side in purchasing necessities, and the wife was thrilled, because for the first time in her life she felt free from her fear of over-spending and enjoyed being able to spend money on things she needed.

What expectations do you have about your marriage? Have you talked them through with your husband? Do you have agreements on how you will deal with money, in-laws, and the discipline of your children?

You will be surprised to see how things can improve if you simply talk to each other. After a heated exchange about Joe's schedule one night, we sat down and talked about our expectations. I told him that I didn't want to feel that I came last after every need at church had been met. We agreed to protect a few nights at home each week and to have one evening that was just ours to spend with each other. When we communicated our expectations and came to an agreement, I no longer felt that Joe was breaking any promises. He fulfilled our agreement and I was happy, even on the nights I spent alone.

## What Do I Have Control Over?

You might be thinking, *That's fine, Martie, and it may work sometimes, but my husband and I have had such conversations and they seem to go in one ear and out the other.* If this is the case, you may feel even worse than before because a spoken promise *has* been broken.

I've found that when this happens, it helps to remind myself about what I can control and what I can't. For example, I know I can't control Joe's actions. If I try to, he'll resent it. He alone has control over what he does. I can try to influence him, I can try to be a resource for him, and I can attempt to provide an environment that makes him want to keep his promises, but he's the one who must follow through.

However, I *can* control my own actions and attitudes

toward my husband. I can choose to be mean and disrespectful when he disappoints me, or I can choose to be forgiving and deferential. I can choose to remain silent as a means of punishing him, or I can choose to talk honestly about how I'm feeling.

I saw the truth of this several years ago when Joe, the eternal optimist, bought a car on credit, claiming he'd pay it off within the year. Well, the year came and went, and we still hadn't paid off that debt. I was upset because I felt that he'd been too optimistic about the money he'd hoped to earn and the amount we could afford to put toward a vehicle.

Yelling at Joe wouldn't have helped us pay off the car any faster, however, nor would it have reflected the love and respect I have for him. It would simply have driven a wedge between us on the issue so he'd be less likely to want to talk about decisions like it in the future. Instead, I chose to talk with him about creating a new plan to pay off the debt while remaining within our budget. I was able to state clearly what I thought should happen, without making him feel like a failure.

Joe's optimism can be a wonderful blessing to our marriage. When it creates a problem, however, rather than trying to control him, I try to control my response. He's different from me, and I'm learning to appreciate his differences.

I would be less than truthful if I led you to believe that I always choose self-control over trying to control my husband. I'm thankful that God expects progress, not perfection. I want our marriage relationship to be built on our mutual love for each other in Jesus Christ, rather than on my nagging or need to control. If I take the path of self-control, I will help our marriage over the long haul.

### How Do I Respond?

Once I've decided to take responsibility for my own actions, I have to determine what my response will be. Most of all I want my responses to Joe to be patterned after my responses to the Lord. God has called me into this marriage, and my vow was to Him, not just to Joe. So when I'm faced with a broken promise, I want to respond the way Paul encourages us to respond in Ephesians 4:29: "Do not let any unwholesome talk come out of your mouths, but only what is helpful for building others up according to their needs, that it may benefit those who listen."

It's easy to let our words get away from us. A few well-timed verbal blasts may seem like the most satisfying way to respond to being hurt, but God calls us to be different. He calls us to use our mouths to build others up, not to tear them down.

So when Joe breaks a promise to me, I do my best to respond in four different ways. First, I use my words as medicine for healing rather than as weapons to attack. When I feel that Joe has broken a promise, I try to tell him how I feel right away rather than bottling it up until it explodes one day. I want to deal with any problem as it arises. When I talk with him about my feelings, I try to speak respectfully and clearly about the specific issue at hand. When I'm angry, it's tempting to bring up every failure my husband has had in twenty-plus years of marriage, but that's not loving or helpful. I do my best to state what I think the problem is without personally attacking him. I feel free to say what I feel, but I'm careful not to be accusatory. Our words don't have to be weapons. They can be tools that move our relationship toward healing.

Second, I try to be tolerant. Paul goes on to say in Ephesians 4, "Be kind and compassionate to one another, forgiving each other, just as in Christ God forgave you" (v. 32). Heaven knows, Joe has been tolerant with me on plenty of occasions! I have my weaknesses, and my husband loves me anyway. So when Joe breaks a promise, I want to be forgiving.

God deals with us from a merciful posture; His arms are open, His words are healing, He wants sinners to return to Him. That's the position I want to reflect when my husband breaks a promise. I want him to know that I still love him, and that I want our relationship to be strong. God has offered me so much more grace than I deserve, yet He is willing to offer me more each time I sin. He issues no threats and holds no grudges. The Lord provides not only forgiveness, but also a chance to grow. That's the model I want to follow.

The third thing I try to remember to do when Joe breaks a promise is pray. Often prayer has kept me from saying something that could have been destructive to our relationship. I can't have the mind of God unless I spend time talking with Him about my situation. I pray for the Lord to give me wisdom, to fill me with love, and to remind me of His forgiveness. Paul also warns us in Ephesians 4 to "not grieve the Holy Spirit of God, with whom you were sealed for the day of redemption" (v. 30). Praying will keep me close to the Lord, which is essential when I'm dealing with a difficult situation.

While I'm praying, I also pray for Joe. Perhaps God is going to use this situation to help him grow, and I want to allow God to work rather than get in His way. When I talk to God about what has happened and how I feel, I'm more likely to see things from His perspective and to remember my desire to be the kind of woman who pleases Him.

Finally, I make every effort to move toward a resolution. Resolution may come as Joe offers an explanation or an apology for his broken promise. Or it may come from our agreeing on a new course of action.

Forgiveness is almost always part of reaching a resolution, even if it's not asked for. To offer forgiveness means to acknowledge that the situation is concluded and I won't bring it up again. "Get rid of all bitterness, rage and anger, brawling and slander," Paul tells us, "along with every form of malice" (Ephesians 4:31). This can be an incredibly difficult assignment for a wife who has experienced a broken promise. But the real heart of the situation is you can either allow the broken promise to hurt your marriage, or you can allow the mercy of God to heal it. Resolution moves you toward a new understanding in your marriage. It gives you both a new place to begin and helps you focus on the future rather than the past.

## What Do I Do with the Painful Feelings?

None of us are robots. You can't help the way you feel, and if you deny your feelings, you'll end up being bitter. If you are deeply hurt, don't repress your emotions. Go to the Lord and pour out your heart. Tell Him you're hurting. God is waiting to meet with you and to offer you His love and healing.

There isn't anything wrong with feeling pain. God made you an emotional being, able to love and able to hurt. Remember, Christ wept when He was hurt over the death of his friend Lazarus. Also, when He heard of his cousin John the Baptist's terrible death, He went to a lonely place to be by Himself. Scripture tells us that the Holy Spirit can also be grieved. Tell the Lord about your pain and ask Him to comfort you.

Every woman also needs a confidant—a pastor, a Christian friend, or a godly adviser to whom she can talk. Often, simply verbalizing your situation to someone can help you deal with it emotionally and move you toward healing. Develop a relationship with someone you trust and can talk to regularly. It will keep you from feeling that you have to dump everything on your husband during the times you have together.

As you express your feelings, be aware of some potential pitfalls:

- Don't be envious of another wife who has a "good" husband.

- Don't wallow in self-pity over broken promises.

- Don't allow pent-up anger to turn you into a bitter person.

All of these responses promote resentment against your husband and have a tendency to deepen the divide between you rather than bring healing and change to your marriage.

Your response to your husband when he breaks a promise will have an impact on your marriage. Your goal should be to reflect Jesus Christ who offered forgiveness to those who crucified Him. Love in the face of a broken promise can bring profound healing and unity to your marriage. Your husband will be strengthened and encouraged to see that you still stand by him, even when he blows it. And you will grow in your walk with God. You will be able to say that you have put God's Word into practice in your life.

Remember, Paul was talking to wives as well as husbands in Colossians 3:12–14 when he said, "Therefore, as God's chosen people, holy and dearly loved, clothe yourselves with compassion, kindness, humility, gentleness and patience. Bear with each other and forgive whatever grievances you may have against one another. Forgive as the Lord forgave you. And over all these virtues put on love, which binds them all together in perfect unity."

I want to be a godly wife who reflects Christ in everything I do. God designed me especially for Joe and put us together as part of His perfect plan. So when Joe fails me in some way, I don't want to allow that failure to derail God's work in our lives. Instead, I want to respond to my husband the same way Jesus Christ would. That is an incredibly difficult thing to do at times because I'm often thinking of my own pain rather than God's plan. The only way I can respond in a Christ-like manner is to remain close to the Lord and learn to rely on His strength.

I encourage you to find comfort and strength in the One who loves you more than any other.

> Do you not know?
> Have you not heard?
> The Lord is the everlasting God,
> the Creator of the ends of the earth.
> He will not grow tired or weary,
> and his understanding no one can fathom.
> He gives strength to the weary
> and increases power of the weak....
> But those who hope in the Lord
> will renew their strength.
> They will soar on wings like eagles;
> they will run and not grow weary,
> they will walk and not be faint.
>                     Isaiah 40: 28–31

**Martie Stowell** resides in Chicago where her husband serves as the president of Moody Bible Institute. She and Joe share the joy of three married children and one grandchild. Martie is active in ministry to student wives and enjoys traveling with her husband, reading, history, and England.

## Questions for Discussion

1. Describe a time within the past month when you felt your husband did not keep a promise. How did you respond? If you could go back and respond differently, what would you do?

2. Who is your confidant when you need to express painful feelings regarding your husband's failure to keep certain promises? Is this person trustworthy to support and help strengthen you and your marriage? Why or why not?

3. Describe a time when your husband's "broken promise" was actually the result of unclear expectations between you. Is there any area that you two should discuss so miscommunication is less likely in the future?

4. What are the things about your husband that you tend to try to control? After reading this chapter, what ideas come to mind regarding where your focus should be?

5. Discuss this statement: "Love in the face of a broken promise can bring profound healing and unity to your marriage." Describe a time when you and your husband experienced this truth.

# CHAPTER TWELVE

Lois Evans

$W$omen often ask me, "How is a woman supposed to find
the time and energy to support her husband, fulfill her own
duties, and still maintain her first love for the Lord?"

I don't have an easy answer for that question; I don't think
there is an easy answer. After years as a pastor's wife, mother
of four, and administrator of a national ministry, I'm still
learning how to balance all of these callings. But God has
taught me some keys to success that might encourage you as
you seek to be the woman He wants you to be.

## Key #1: Let God Set Your Priorities

As I look back on my life, I see a trend. When I am doing
what God wants me to do, I can get it all done with an inner
sense of joy and energy. But when I do just what I want to do or
what others demand that I do, I am joyless and lack stamina.
I believe this is because God only obligates Himself to His

agenda, not to mine. Therefore, the more time I spend in His presence learning His will, the more productive I become in what He wants me to accomplish. The more I pursue Him, the clearer His will becomes to me and the more I function as His woman. It is up to me to drop the things from my life that are not part of what He wants me to do.

In 1 Corinthians 10:13, God promises that He will not give us more to handle than we can bear. The issue is not whether we women can do it all; the issue is doing only those things God has called us to do. No woman can do everything, but she can do everything God wants her to do because He will never burden her with too much.

My faith in that promise was tested when at fifteen I gladly surrendered my life to full-time ministry. I had always wanted to be married and share in ministry with my husband, but there was one role I told the Lord I never wanted to fill: pastor's wife. After watching the way pastors' wives seemed to have so many demands and expectations put upon them by so many people, I determined I would never be a pastor's wife. My perceptions were not entirely accurate, but that's the way I saw things.

Well, as you can see, God definitely has a sense of humor! I married Tony Evans in 1970, and in 1976 we started the Oak Cliff Bible Fellowship with ten people in our home. I struggled to accept what God's will was for me. Obviously, if Tony was called to be a pastor, I was called to be a pastor's wife. I said yes to that call because of the commitment I'd made to the Lord as a teenager and because of my commitment to Tony. But it was still hard for me to get used to the idea that I was going to be a pastor's wife who would be expected to be all things to all people.

I did everything: played the piano, started the choir, taught the kids, met with the women, and whatever else had to be done. Because I was in His will, God gave me the ability to get the job done without compromising my priorities. Whenever I compromised my priorities, the joy of ministry left and so did the ability and the power to accomplish it. So, I had to learn early that the key to balancing a lot of responsibilities is to make my walk with God my number-one priority so that He can help me prioritize my responsibilities in life.

During those early years as a pastor's wife, Tony was a great help and encouragement to me. He prayed for me and said he wasn't asking me to be whatever the people in the church wanted me to be. He only wanted me to use my gifts and abilities alongside him in the ministry. That really freed me up. It also helped to realize that I was the pastor's wife, not the church's wife. The more I realized this, the more I focused on what God had called me and gifted me to do and not on what others perceived I should be doing.

God enabled me to grow into my role, and when the demand for Tony's ministry started to grow, I began to help meet the need by taking on several administrative duties at The Urban Alternative, a Christian ministry that seeks to help churches rebuild their cities from the inside out. Because I had spent time alone with Him, I knew that God was calling me to use my administrative gifts, skills, and training to organize, set up, and lead the ministry that He would use to bring His Word to hundreds of thousands of people. Since then I've also been blessed to see how God has used Tony to encourage Christian men across the country through the Promise Keepers movement, and to know that I had a strategic part to play.

## Key #2: Remember That Everything Has a Season

Another crucial key to maintaining your love for God while meeting life's many obligations is remembering that everything has a season (Ecclesiastes 3:1). God doesn't want us to do it all now.

Sometimes when my children were young I got frustrated that I wasn't using my administrative abilities outside the home. But it just wasn't my season yet. God's first priority was for me to focus on my kids. I can remember women getting upset because I declined their invitations to speak at their churches and retreats. But as my children grew older and started school, God opened up doors and created new desires that matched those opportunities. My season had changed.

It is important that we love God in whatever season is upon us rather than simply complain. Sooner or later, spring will replace the cold of winter, and fall will replace the heat of summer, as God moves us into new opportunities that fit His will for us in the changing seasons of life. If we try to change seasons on our own, then we might remove ourselves from His will. As a result we will lose our peace, power, and productivity.

## Key #3: Develop a Noble, Christ-like Character

As I prayed about the content of this chapter and thought about how a Christian wife can do all the things she needs to do, a biblical image came to mind: the "wife of noble character" in Proverbs 31:10–31. If we women are going to see ourselves in the proper light, we need to shine the light of God's Word on our lives.

The woman described in Proverbs 31 definitely embodies the spiritual qualities and gifts that would allow one to fulfill any role God might call her to fill. As we will see, this woman was a pillar of support to her husband: she served and loved him and her family while serving and loving the Lord, yet she also fully developed the gifts and abilities God had given her.

I realize that for many women today, the Proverbs 31 woman is almost too perfect, too much of an ideal. But I don't believe God put this profile in His Word to frustrate women and make us feel like we can't measure up. Although the details and particulars of your life and mine may vary greatly from hers, this portrait of a godly woman, wife, mother, and businesswoman is one that the Holy Spirit invites you and me to strive for in His power. So let's see what God's Word has to teach us.

We almost need to start at the end of the chapter, because verse 30 is the key to what enables a woman to fulfill her God-given roles. The key to this woman's life and accomplishments was that they flowed out of a heart that was anchored in God. This doesn't just mean that she went to church; it means she had integrated her relationship with God into every aspect of her life, with the result that God empowered her for everything He was expecting her to do. Remember, the busier you are, the more you need God. And because this woman feared the Lord, every area of her life was affected by her walk with Him. Whenever our many commitments and activities (even spiritual ones) cause our love for Christ to wane, we must immediately pause and reflect on what adjustments must be made to reignite the fire.

Do you remember the television commercial in which a well-dressed woman sang a tune that went something like this: "I can bring home the bacon, fry it up in a pan, and never let you forget you are a man, because I'm a woman"?

That was a song of liberation, a song that said, "I can do it all!"

But you see, that's nothing new. The woman of Proverbs 31 did all of the things suggested in that song, and did them right. But it wasn't because she was some kind of "super-woman" who didn't need anybody else.

The feminist movement of the past thirty years has given us many angry, frustrated women who are still trying to prove to themselves, and especially to men, that they can do it all, do it better, and do it without any help. But in Proverbs 31 we see a woman who achieved more than most feminists will ever achieve, yet did so in the context of a loving home and family and unswerving devotion to the Lord.

The message to women is clear: What we need is liberation, but with biblical application. This gives us true liberty without focusing on the oppression of women and fierce competition between the sexes. Instead of focusing on inequity, competition, and bitterness, the writer of Proverbs 31 begins his profile of the godly woman by looking into the home, at a marriage where the wife is a person of noble character. "Who can find" such a woman? "She is worth far more than rubies" (v. 10). Here the writer lets us know something that ought to be a real boost to your sense of self-worth as a Christian woman and wife: This noble woman is someone who is worthy of the honor paid to a queen.

If you seek to please the Lord, love and support your husband, and use your God-given abilities to strengthen your home and advance the work of God, you are "rare." God is looking for a woman like this just as much as a man may be looking for one to be his partner.

Notice that even though a woman like this is rare, the

standard is not impossible for you and me to reach. If the main criterion of a woman's worth in God's sight was her physical beauty, then obviously only the most beautiful women among us could meet the requirements. But God looks on the heart (1 Samuel 16:7). With dependency on the power of the indwelling Holy Spirit, you can achieve the noble character God desires.

Verse 11 says, "Her husband has full confidence in her and lacks nothing of value." This is a great contrast to the "battle between the sexes" and the lack of trust that marks so many marriages. The opposite of supporting your husband is to do and say things that break the trust between you.

Marriage is such an intimate relationship that it is easy for one partner to harm the other. As a husband and wife share their lives, they both gain intimate knowledge that needs to be held in complete trust not because these things are wrong, but because they are private. A wife in particular understands the power of these things, and she can be tempted to use them against her husband when she's angry. When a husband breaks this kind of trust, it takes a woman of extraordinary character not to retaliate, destroying trust further.

## Key #4: *Make Home Your Primary Focus*

A good portion of the remaining verses of Proverbs 31 deal with this noble woman's work in the home, in the market-place, and in the community. She was a capable business-woman as well as being a wife and mother.

Of course, this always raises the question of whether or not Scripture permits godly wives and mothers to work outside the home. This is a question that cannot be adequately answered with a simple *yes* or *no*. I say that because the Bible

193

doesn't make the answer that clear. For example, it's evident that the woman of Proverbs 31 was accomplished in business, dealing in textiles, making garments, and buying and selling real estate. She was also a very frugal and resourceful shopper. But her business didn't cause her to neglect her family. Far from it. Verses 15 and 21–28 testify to her care for her family, and she even had time to minister to the needy outside her home (v. 20).

This woman illustrates the biblical principle that governs the choice of outside activities for a wife and mother: these things are permissible as long as they don't take priority over her primary responsibility of caring for her family. The Apostle Paul tells us that a wife's primary focus is to be on the home (Titus 2:5). Many women resist this because they think being a "keeper" at home means being a "stayer" at home. But Paul is not telling women to stay home and never venture out for any other commitments. The issue is their priorities and the impact of their outside activities on their home.

This is one place where the Proverbs 31 woman is a far cry from many of her twentieth–century sisters. The annals of American business are filled with stories of women who are stressed out, overworked, and absent from home. Unfortunately, since many of these women are also wives and mothers, their families are paying a terrible price.

Obviously, the culture of Proverbs 31 is also a far cry from modern America. This woman worked out of her home, so she was also available to her family. Many people would say that this "ideal" situation isn't possible today. But more and more women are finding creative ways to carry on their outside work while being at home, and we can hope this trend will increase.

Either way, it is still possible for you and me to obey the

principles of Scripture concerning our outside activities. The writer of Proverbs 31 never says that we need to be merchants, expert seamstresses, real estate buyers, or market traders to be women of nobility. This particular woman had these abilities, but they may not be your areas of expertise. The principle of the Scripture is that the wise use of your gifts in their season qualifies you for the title of noble wife. Many women will say that their commitment to the Lord, to their husbands, and to their children is the way they maximize their gifts.

There's another reason that the question of a woman working outside the home cannot be answered with a simple *yes* or *no*. That's because the answer may differ at different stages in a family's life. In our case, when Tony entered Dallas Seminary, we had two small children and no extra money. Tony was going to be a full-time student, but he still felt responsible to provide for our family. And we both knew the kids needed me to be home. So we made a commitment before the Lord that I would not work, and we would get by on the $350 a month Tony was able to bring home working part-time.

I remember when Tony prayed, "Lord, the only way this is going to work is if You supply our need. We have made a spiritual decision that Lois needs to be home. But Father, with $350 a month I can't make it. So Lord, if it's Your will that I go to school and Lois stay home with our children, the only way we'll make it is if You intervene."

Those were hard times financially. When your monthly income is $350, your rent is $170, and your tithe is $50, something has to give. But we watched God meet our needs in miraculous ways again and again. And I was able to be with our children full-time.

Then as the church and the ministry of The Urban Alternative began to grow, I sensed God's call to come alongside Tony, as I mentioned earlier. One key for me in this decision was that Tony was supportive of it, and we didn't view it as trading my home responsibilities for my responsibilities in the ministry, especially since our kids were now in school.

## Key #5: Have a Servant's Heart

The Proverbs 31 woman evidently ran a well-to-do household in the context of that culture. In verse 15 we learn that she had servants. Does this fact separate this woman from those of us who don't have household help? Many women would say, "Well, no wonder she could do all those things; she had servants to do the daily tasks." But when you factor in the modern conveniences we enjoy today such as washing machines, dryers, vacuum cleaners, and dishwashers, and realize that the simplest daily jobs were very time-consuming in the ancient world, you see that our home workload isn't that different from hers.

This woman may have had servants, but she also had a servant attitude. According to verse 15, she prepared the morning meal for her servant girls as well as her family. That seems a little backward, doesn't it? Isn't that what servants are for, to prepare meals and bring them to you? But this woman evidently valued people. She understood that if she invested in her servants, they would invest in her. These servants were more than just people who worked for her; they were people she cared about.

This is another key to a woman's ability to do all the things we've been talking about: She must have the heart of a servant because that's the kind of heart God honors. The woman in Proverbs 31 was not bound to a form of household slavery in which she was overworked and under-appreciated by her family. On the contrary, this woman's husband honored her spirit and her commitment by making it easier, not harder, for her to accomplish her tasks.

I don't know what the specific application of this principle might be in your home, but if you are standing by your man in love and support, God is free to work in his heart and show him how to honor your commitment.

## Key #6: Take Care of Yourself

By this time you may be thinking, *Goodness, any woman who can do all this must be worn out and look pretty haggard.* But according to verse 22, the wife of noble character also takes care of herself.

This is an interesting verse because we women have a lot of people today telling us to take care of ourselves first, not to allow a husband or a family to keep us from "self-fulfillment." This is not the kind of self-care that Proverbs 31 is talking about, however. Again, this woman does not neglect her family to lavish attention on herself. But she understands that to minister to others effectively, she must also care for the temple of her own body. And her family has a lot to do with this, because a husband and children can love and support a woman in such a way that her inner and outer beauty are enhanced rather than depreciated.

Tony often says to husbands, "It's a tragedy for your wife to be less beautiful today than the day you married her. Now I don't mean she has to try to look like she's twenty or thirty years younger than she actually is. But if you load down your wife with a bunch of responsibilities and demands and then talk about how bad she looks, that's your fault! It's your responsibility to make sure that your wife is so well cared for that all of the beauty she possesses is enhanced. A woman can grow more lovely with the passing of years as she acquires godly character and a gentle spirit. Husbands, what are you doing to help your wives develop and maintain that kind of beauty?"

## Key #7: Recognize Your Need for Support

The issue of a woman fulfilling the roles God gives her is not a one-sided matter. That's really what I've been saying all along. No woman can do it all by herself; neither can any man. And that's not what God asks us to do. He provides the strength for us to fulfill our responsibilities as husbands and wives as we love and support one another.

One result of the Proverbs 31 woman's noble character is the respect her husband attains at the "city gate" (v. 23). He is able to take his place among "the elders of the land." The city gate was the equivalent of downtown today. It was where business was transacted and civic decisions were made. This woman's husband was so well-known because he was so well taken care of by his noble wife. And he let everyone know it (v. 28).

When Tony preaches on Proverbs 31, men always ask him afterward, "How can I get my wife to be like the woman in Proverbs 31?" Tony always points them to verse 28. The idea is, husbands, if you want a Proverbs 31 wife, you need to be a Proverbs 31 husband.

I don't know how many of my sisters in Christ are starving for a little praise and attention from their husbands, but I suspect their number is legion. Most wives don't need a parade downtown in their honor; they just want to hear their husbands affirm them and lift them up. Look what the Proverbs

31 husband says to wife: "Many women do noble things, but you surpass them all" (v. 29). I can't imagine a wife who wouldn't flourish under that kind of genuine praise.

I like what Tony says about this, so allow me to quote him again: "Gentlemen, you need to tell your wife, 'Honey, my life is only worth living because I have the privilege of living it with you! My greatest joy tomorrow will be to wake up and find you to be the first thing I see when I open my eyes.'"

I suspect that if every Christian husband got up tomorrow morning and said something like that to his wife, many wives would go into shock or wonder what was in his coffee! But the fact that this kind of praise sounds like hyperbole only shows how little effort we as husbands and wives put into praising and lifting up our mates.

Women can be very vulnerable on this point. The reason many women enter illicit affairs is not just for the sexual adventure, but because some man is smooth with his words and lavish in his praise. If a woman is hungry enough for affirmation, she can fall for a man's lines. We women need to guard our hearts, and husbands need to keep their promises at home.

## Keeping God First

We are now back where we started, at verse 30. A woman's spiritual life is the anchor, the foundation that holds all of life together. When a woman fears the Lord, when her spiritual priorities are in place and she integrates God into every area of her life, she will have a well of strength, joy, and peace to draw on that will never run dry. Yes, she will grow weary at times. She will feel overwhelmed by the responsibilities placed upon her. But when she is connected to Christ, He will renew her day by day.

So, then, what must we as women do to keep our first love for the Lord fresh? First of all, we must not let anything take the place of our daily time in God's presence. A disciplined devotional life is crucial if we desire to stay close to the Savior and be in a position to receive His strength to face the many demands that we are called to face. As Jesus told Martha, it is better to do less for Him that we might develop more intimacy *with* Him (Luke 10:38–42).

Second, make sure you are fulfilling God's calling on your life and not simply satisfying the expectations of people. While we must be sensitive to people, we are called to follow the Lord. At the judgment seat of Christ, the issue will not be, *How many people did we please?* but rather, *How much did we please the Lord?* When this latter concern dominates our lives, then we will not so easily succumb to the expectations and demand of others. We will just run their demands through the grid of how they fit into God's calling on our life. If they don't fit, we can then say *no*, in love, without feeling guilty. Many women live unfulfilled lives because they are doing things God never asked them to do.

The third way to keep God first is to maintain biblical priorities. As I said earlier, anything we're involved in outside of our home that competes or conflicts with God's priority of our family must be either readjusted or released. It's amazing how many Christian men and women want to fix the world but are unwilling to fix their families first. After our family, our priority should be involvement in the ministry of our local church. A good church provides the spiritual reinforcement, fellowship, and support we need to keep our lives on track. Our third priority should be serving others outside our family and church, not only to contribute to the wellbeing of our community, but also to share our faith with the unsaved.

The joy and empowerment of the Lord comes only when we are falling in love with His purposes, not getting Him to adjust to ours. Let me ask you a question in closing: Does your inner beauty shine through for everyone to see? If charm and physical beauty are not the defining characteristics of a godly woman, then what is the condition of your soul? Can God say of you, "Here is a woman of noble character"? When God can say that, then you are ready for the reward of His commendation, "Well done, good and faithful servant! You have been faithful with a few things; I will put you in charge of many things. Come and share your master's happiness!" (Matthew 25:21).

A woman like this can say to even the most rigorous feminist, "I have what you're looking for. I have a family, fulfilling work, satisfaction, and peace of heart. I have a husband whom I love and who loves me. My children are well cared for. I have confidence in the present, and I know where I'm going in the future. Now, what are you offering me?"

This is the woman of noble character. Her spirit is in tune with her Lord; she is secure in who she is; she receives the praise of her family; and she has her priorities in order. May God help us all to be women like this as we stand by our men.

**Lois Evans** is the executive assistant to the president of the Urban Alternative, an outreach ministry. She earned her BA in Business Administration from Dallas Baptist University. Her accomplishments include recording two vocal albums, serving for twenty years as a pastor's wife, and rearing four children. She is married to her favorite pastor, teacher, and best friend, Dr. Tony Evans.

## Questions for Discussion

1. Do you agree that when you're doing what God wants you to do, you have plenty of energy and joy? Why or why not? Is there anything you're doing that is causing you to feel drained and depressed?

2. What "season" of your life are you in right now: winter, spring, summer, or fall? How can you settle comfortably into this season and maintain a passionate love for God?

3. Is there any area of your life in which you have not fully integrated God? How can you more strongly anchor yourself in Him in this area so you can experience His power and energy?

4. In what ways is the example of the woman in Proverbs 31 relevant to your life today? In what areas do you want to follow her example more closely? What are some specific actions you can take?

5. In what ways do your husband and children support you in fulfilling your God-given role? In what ways do you feel that God sustains you amidst your many responsibilities?

OTHER BOOKS FROM

# *Vision House Publishing*

### *Stories for the Heart:* 110 Stories to Encourage Your Soul

Compiled by Alice Gray, ISBN 1-885305-41-9, Retail $10.99 (trade paper)

This book offers readers heart-warming stories about love, friendship and heaven to refresh the spirit. Included are stories from Max Lucado, Billy Graham, Chuck Swindoll, Paul Harvey and others.

### *Women of Honor:* God's Incredible Plan for Fulfillment

Jeanne Hendricks, ISBN 1-885305-13-3, Retail $17.99 (hardback)

Discover the priceless privilege of womanhood as God intended. You will be encouraged and uplifted as you discover your worth to God.

### *Acts of Love:* The Power of Encouragement

David Jeremiah, ISBN 1-885305-00-1, Retail $17.99 (hardback)

Real love is shown through encouraging others and most often the individual who is freely giving encouragement is the one most blessed.

### *Marriage:* Experience the Best

Steve Stephens, ISBN 1-885305-12-5, Retail $13.99 (paperback)

Look at marriage through your partner's eyes—communicating and loving by understanding.

### *Standing Together:* Impacting Your Generation

Howard Hendricks, ISBN 1-885305-31-1, Retail $17.99 (hardback)

Learn what it takes to be a true servant leader and how to pass your ministry on to the next generation.

### *Real Family Values:* Keeping the Faith in an Age of Cultural Chaos

Robert Lewis with Rich Cambell, ISBN 1-885305-22-2, Retail $17.99 (hardback)

Prepare your loved ones for the bold new world and instill a vision for godliness in your family with courage, compassion and discernment.

### *First Hand Faith:* Secrets of Raising Godly Children

Bruce Wilkinson, ISBN 1-885305-37-0, Retail $17.99 (hardback)

Before parents can create a spiritual legacy for their children they need to get themselves in what the author calls the "first chair" position with God.

### Purchasing Information

Books are available from your favorite bookstore. If they don't carry inventory, you can assist them in ordering by giving them the author and ISBN number. If you are unable to purchase from your local bookstore, you may order directly from Vision House Publishing by calling (503) 492-0200 — We accept both Visa and Mastercard. Or make checks payable to Vision House Publishing for the full amount of the title plus $3.00 shipping and handling and send them to, 1217 NE Burnside Road, Suite 403, Gresham, Oregon, 97030, Attn. Customer Service (US Funds only please). Please remember to indicate title or titles you wish to purchase.